THEY BUILT RAILWAY CARS

The Pullman Social Experiment

and

the Swedish Immigration

Allan T. Nilson

English Translation from Swedish of
De Byggde Järnvägsvagnar
(They Built Railway Cars)

by

Raymond E. Johnson

Heritage Books
2025

HERITAGE BOOKS
AN IMPRINT OF HERITAGE BOOKS, INC.

Books, CDs, and more—Worldwide

For our listing of thousands of titles see our website
at
www.HeritageBooks.com

A Facsimile Reprint
Published 2025 by
HERITAGE BOOKS, INC.
Publishing Division
5810 Ruatan Street
Berwyn Heights, MD 20740

Copyright © 2002 Raymond E. Johnson, translator

De Byggde Järnvägsvagnar
by Allan T. Nilson
Originally published in Swedish
by Tre Bocker Forlag

— Publisher's Notice —
In reprints such as this, it is often not possible to remove
blemishes from the original. We feel the contents of this
book warrant its reissue despite these blemishes and
hope you will agree and read it with pleasure.

International Standard Book Number
Paperbound: 978-0-7884-2076-4

Contents

Translator's Foreword v
Author's Preface vii
Introduction, The Project ix
I   Purpose Defined 1
II   Swedes Who Lived and Worked in Pullman 7
III   The Elim Congregation 23
IV   Natives of Ryfors at Home and Abroad 39
V   The Town of Pullman: "Villages of Vision" 55
VI   In the Shadow of the Metropolis 65
VII Their Employer; The Strike! 75
VIII Their Job; Coaches and Trains 86
IX   My Conclusion 101
Sources, Periodicals, Literature 107
Supplement: Emigrants From Nykyrke Parish 1850-1910 115
Index 121
About the Author ....

Translator's Foreword

Allan T. Nilson's book about the Swedish emigration to Pullman in the 1880s is written in the Swedish language and is aimed at readers in Western Sweden where the majority of the immigrants originated. As he states in the opening of Chapter 2, he advertised in Swedish journals as well as in some Swedish-American publications in the United States. His purpose was to gather accounts of personal experiences of those who came and those who stayed behind, from their letters and the memories of their descendants.

The day I answered his advertisement in *The Bridge*, was one that altered the routine of my life and marked the beginning of a five-year correspondence; he writing in Swedish, I in English. In my answer I informed him that all of my grandparents were among those who came from Sweden to live and work in Pullman. Allan replied with enthusiasm and a barrage of questions. In each following letter my first task was to translate his impatient scrawl, then to find answers for him. Every reply came with effusive thanks and more questions.

When the project was completed and copies of the book in my hands, I chose chapters two and three for an initial translation because they contained material likely to be of immediate interest to the South Suburban Genealogical and Historical Society (Chicago) for their value in genealogical research and to the Historic Pullman Foundation as an addition to their archival material. The two chapters were published in January, 2000 by SSG&HS. Then with the same purpose in mind I undertook translation of the complete book with hope that the fascinating story and wealth of genealogical data will be of widespread interest.

The chapter endnotes are mine. They are intended as additional points of view and supporting information from my own research.

I wish to express my profound thanks to Janice Helge of South Suburban Genealogical & Historical Society and Historic Pullman Foundation for her generous cooperation, interest, and inestimable help in the research that contributed to Allan T. Nilson's book, and for her role as mover-shaker in the writing of this translation.

Raymond E. Johnson
Westminster, Colorado

Author's Preface

During my rather long life I have had, concurrent with my service as a museum man, antiquary, and museum director, many research opportunities within the craft; technical and ethnological. My essays and books have dealt with such emigrations as Scandinavians in Australia and Swedes in New England.

When, at one time, I was advisor to the Swedish-American Museum at Andersonville in Chicago, I found the topic that I am presenting here on G. M. Pullman, his famous railroad cars, technical innovations, and ideal town. Many Swedes lived and worked there, and among the most skilled were immigrants from Ryfors near Mullsjö.

When I now venture to publish some studies from their world, which is expanded in Donald L. Miller, *The City of the Century* 1966, I raise a number of questions on the topic, but naturally I am conscious that an investigation is never completely finished.

But first, I wish to thank those whose contributions have been particularly significant to the study which now comes to print.

Author Raymond E. Johnson, of Chicago and engineer Tage Åkerberg, of Anneberg; the one grew up in the town of Pullman, the other in Ryfors.

Professors Ulf Beijbom, Jan Hult, Björn Linn; Museum Director Lasse Brunnström and Museum Curator Lars Olof Lööf; Docents Gösta Arvastson, Gunilla Linde Bjur, Bertil Rehnberg; and not the least, my wife, Brita, who has been my conversation partner. Professor Bengt Berglund; Docents Lars Ljungmark and Lennart K. Persson; Archivist Bengt O. T. Sjögren have, besides advising, assisted with critical reading.

My rope-making friend, Börje Johansson, Director of the museum at Carlmark's renovated rope-makers' yard in Älvängen, has helped me with my transcriptions.

I have also had the advantage of obtaining a grant for printing from the Royal Gustav Adolf's Academy for Swedish folk Culture, Herbert and Karin Jacobsson Foundation, Wilhelm and Martina Lundgren Support Fund, The Royal Hvitfeldtska Foundation, ek.dr h.c. Erik Malmsten and Director Stefan Gelkner. With all my heart I thank them all.

The book is dedicated to my grandchildren, Tove, Björn, Henrik, and Erik.

Göteborg and Skara, Midsummer Day 1999
Allan T. Nilson

Introduction

The Project

The visit

As I ease my car along the O'Hare Kennedy Expressway, I proceed eastward from "The Loop," pass the University of Chicago, and turn off at 111th Street, Exit 66A, into the town of Pullman. In a moment the Hotel Florence is before me. There I can park the car, go in and eat lunch or brunch which is still served in its Queen Anne atmosphere. After lunch I go up a stairway and visit the museum dedicated to the great man, G. M. Pullman. I buy a copy of the "Blue Buder Book."[1]

Then it is time for a walk through the town, and thanks to the book's index I can orient myself to the region. I see the ongoing restoration work everywhere. No razing of the 1880s row houses can be seen. Instead a program has been approved for the protection and preservation of the surroundings and individual important buildings.[2] The renovation will be carried out carefully so that the buildings' distinctive features are preserved and its cultural history, its environmental and artistic values are taken into account. As soon as the houses were put in order they were occupied. Behind in the gardens I had glimpses of people and the newly-planted flower beds were colorful and neat.[3]

But in years past visitors saw no such pleasant sights full of life and activity. The large dilapidated industrial buildings just to the north are reminders of that period. But these also will undergo a protection program, as it states in the information pamphlet. For a complete understanding of the town of Pullman we must include the industrial region, actually the indispensable part.

I then concluded that the town of Pullman, after a long period of decline, had a cultural heritage worth preserving. At first glance into this past time, one is struck by the high quality of residential facilities. He then considers this along with the technical and industrial craft that was of fundamental importance, "the hub of the wheel," because the power to keep all this going demands a collective opinion and political recognition of the value of preservation.

The book's advent

Now I wanted to learn more about the area, the people, the dwellings, the factories, the enterprise, the labor organizations, the technology, and the changes. And I wanted specific knowledge of the workers' occupations–of those who built the famous Pullman cars. But now all their voices have been silenced. Too many years have passed since the occupational skills flourished, and since the workers and their families lived in these houses.

Therefore it becomes necessary during the writing to make well defined and concentrated research decisions around which the different chapters can be constructed. The entrance of new material may give some clue to the pattern that will be made clearer.

Several years have now gone by since I turned into the 111th Street entrance to G. M. Pullman's town, but its impression remains. And the intentions I tried to follow–to focus on *chosen parts* of the town's and the workers' histories, will also provide a Swedish base and show that many Swedes lived and had been operative in the town of Pullman. Thus my project has been formed in this way:

Summary

In the first chapter, "Purpose Defined," I described how I came upon my material in Chicago, the research material and questions I put to it, the ideas which emerged, and the definitions I made.

In the second chapter I concentrated on two families from Sweden working and living in the town of Pullman and I looked at the town and the enterprise from a microperspective.

In the third chapter I considered information on the Elim Congregation of the town to demonstrate how the Swedish group fitted in.

In the fourth chapter, "Natives of Ryfors at Home and Abroad," I took a closer look at this club of carpenters from Ryfors, Mullsjö, and at the "Ryfors-Pullman emigration axis."

In the fifth chapter, "The Town of Pullman," I witnessed how the town as an ideal community from its advent later suffered a severe period of decline and at present is going through restoration. "A cultural heritage worth saving." For comparison I also presented similar model communities, principally Klippan in Gothenburg.

In the sixth chapter, "In the Shadow of a Metropolis–[a Macroperspective]," I began by making comparisons with the labor situation of Swedes in another city that I had studied, New Britain, Connecticut, in the shadow of its capital city, Hartford. Most of my attention is naturally devoted to Chicago, "The City of the Century." Among events there in the 1890s the "Columbian Exposition" is of great importance to all categories.

In the seventh chapter, "Their Employer; The Strike!," I focused on characteristics of the great enterprise mostly culled from the Pullman Journal, things like "terms, jingles, hints," or how some groups were favored at the expense of others who were neglected. Here the Pullman strike of 1894 was also given its due attention.

In the eighth chapter I opened with the entrepreneur, G. M. Pullman, his innovations, and "Alle Züge nach Chicago,"[4] and I drew comparisons, especially at the department where the Swedes worked, the carpenter car builders.

The ninth chapter combined results with closing commentary and answers to questions that had been posed earlier. My research focus was on the contribution of young men who came from the area west of Lake Vättern.

---

[1] Stanley Buder, *An Experiment in Industrial Order and Community Planning, 1880-1930* (New York: Oxford University Press, 1967)

[2] In 1969 Pullman received State of Illinois landmark status; South Pullman (original housing from 111th Street to 115th Street including factories north of 111th Street to 109th Place along Cottage Grove Avenue).
In 1971 the entire Pullman district (103rd Street to 115th Street) received National Registry designation.
In 1972 South Pullman (109th Place to 115th Street, Cottage Grove to Langley) received City of Chicago Landmark status.
From timeline in: Frank Beberdick, *Chicago's Historic Pullman District,* (Charleston, SC: Arcadia Publishing, 1998) pp. 125-6

[3] In 1898 the Illinois Supreme Court ordered the Pullman Company to sell all property not used for industry. After extensive litigation, the company began selling the homes in 1907. They have been privately owned ever since and all remodeling was done privately.

[4] All railroads lead to Chicago.

Chapter I

Purpose Defined

My project is comprised of studies; of the town of Pullman, records, archive material; of inquiries, particularly from The Newberry Library, Chicago, and from Elim Church in Pullman, Chicago, Illinois.

Some of the printed materials that came from general background material are: Ulf Beijbom's *Swedes in Chicago*, 1971; *Swedish-American Life in Chicago*, eds. Philip J. Anderson and Dag Blanck, 1991; Anita R. Olson's *Swedish Chicago 1880-1920*, 1990; and my own earlier printed studies from the USA, 1975 and 1988, together with those in the works mentioned.

I will begin here with a few brief selections which give a quick glimpse of Pullman and the town of Pullman. They raise questions which will be considered.

E. von Hesse-Wartegg in *North America in Our Day*, 1880, p 268.

> Three factories that make similar sleeping cars may be found within the United States: Pullman, the oldest and largest on western railroads, Wagner in the Northeast, and Woodruff in the southern part of the country.

Karl Jørgensen in *Højskolebladet*, 1885, p. 860.

> In 1880 Pullman secretly bought 3500 acres of land on the west shore of Lake Calumet and immediately began to build his enormous railway car factory and its connected workers' town.

P. Waldenström in *Through North America's United States*, 1891, p. 347.

> Saturday, July 6th. In the evening I preached in Pullman, another suburb of Chicago. It was among the most remarkable phenomena that I had occasion to see in America. I know nothing so typical of the speed of American business as is shown in the history of this town.

Henrik Carling in *Fra Amerika*, 1897, p. 239.

> With smoking, sleeping, and observation cars are also found the Pullman salon-kitchen, and the finely conditioned parlor car and dining car.

August Palm in *A Trip to America*, 1901, p. 112.

> I was also in the notorious town of Pullman which has 12,000 inhabitants who all work in the Pullman factories. There I met groups from various parts of Sweden. Pullman was the patriarch, his workers had not the slightest appeal in their subjection to his will and decision; they were treated, in short, as children until they could no longer contain themselves and their patience would at sometime burst.

F. U. Wrangel in *Class Struggle in New York and Other States*, 1907, p. 104.

> The Americans may be proud of their Pullman cars with good reason, but how it is with the safety of their railroads is another question....

G. H. von Koch in *The Emigrants' Land*, 1910, p. 213.

> Perhaps the most celebrated case in this respect happened during the great Pullman strike when the Republicans' present presidential candidate, the then Judge Taft, prevented the boycott of the railroads by sending one of Debs' assistants to prison for six months.

The subject, material, and questions

The more detailed information encountered in Anita R. Olson's dissertation is of particular interest when she deals with the town of Pullman in several places. Ulf Beijbom, however, has nothing in the way of information about Pullman or the neighboring Roseland in any of his USA books.

The town of Pullman was built in 1880-1881. It was planned to contain everything for the workers at George M. Pullman's Palace Car Company, from the factory and dwellings to the hotel, bank, shops, hospital, church, and schools.

The best known buildings were: The clock tower, Hotel Florence, executive housing, workers' cottages, Colonnade Apartments, Market Hall, block houses, three-flat apartments, bay front apartments, boarding house, skilled craftsmen housing, Pullman Hospital, Greenstone Church, row houses, Pullman stables, The Arcade, and foreman's row.

The town and factory were designed by the architect, Solon Spencer Beman, and Nathan F. Barret was the landscape architect who designed the surrounding parks.

Pullman left the entire responsibility to Beman, that is, to make the plans and design the houses and factories.

Parallels to Pullman's vision may be found, as examples, in Henry Acland's *Health, Work, and Play*, 1856, and *Health in the Village*, 1884; in James Holes' *Homes of the Working Classes With Suggestions For Their improvement*, 1866; in Robert Owen's *Report to the County of Lanark*, 1821, and *A New View of Society*, 1813-14; and in Henry Roberts' *Dwellings of the Labouring Classes*, 1850.

We also have a parallel in Gothenburg in the Klippan region, where, in the 1850 decade, David Carnegie Jr. built a porter brewery, workers homes, school, chapel, managers' homes, bakery, offices, doctor consulting room, and much more. All are in an enclosed area and in the Scottish style of building.

Architects with similar vision in England were William H. Lever, Joseph Rowntree, and Henrietta Barnett, among others. Lever's work is Port Sunlight from the 1880s. Still earlier were Saltaire from 1861, and Bournville, originated in the 1870s with dwellings in groups some distance from the industrial complex.

Among several authors whose penetrating questions on this subject can be pointed out are: Gillian Darley's *Villages of Vision*, 1975, which resembles B. Meakins' *Model Factories and Villages: Ideal Conditions of Labour and Housing*, 1905, G. Atterbury's *Model Towns in America*, 1912, Dolores Hayden's *Seven American Utopias*, 1976, Helen Rosenau's *The Ideal City*, 1959, and J. B. Lowe's *Welsh Industrial Workers' Housing*, 1977.

How then, did George Mortimer Pullman get his ideas to build his ideal town? It becomes, accordingly, one of the questions we must pose and look for the answer.

Pullman was one of the great innovators within the railroad industry. Several of his technical achievements have indirectly influenced our Swedish rail traffic. In railroad talk one speaks of Pullman cars as a concept of salon cars with sleeping places that open and swing down, and Pullman cars for expensive luxury trains. He was also one of the men behind the changing of railroad cars from the composite stagecoach to a vehicle with railroad-specific design.

Pullman planned his factories and cars with his economic advisor, Col. James H. Bowen, and above all, as we have seen, with his architect, Solon Spencer Beman.

The construction of improved railroad cars was principally the teamwork of Pullman himself and his personal friend Benjamin C. Field at the head. With money from a building enterprise in Chicago and with the help of several carpenters, they built, without prepared drawings, a sleeping car with the upholstered seats that became the Pullman car's mark of distinction.

After the Civil War they began what would become "The Pioneer" with comfortable seats in walnut that became the lower beds; with wash stands of marble, and with upper beds which were folded against the ceiling in the daytime. The sleeping places were separated by draperies. In 1867 they built the first hotel car and in 1868 "The Delmonico," the first restaurant car. In 1887 they constructed the first so-called bellows coupling which made passage between cars safer.

The improved sleeping car types, "Majestic" and "Teutonic" were placed on the rail route between Chicago and St. Louis. The undercarriages of these cars were of the bogie construction, an innovation that spread over the entire world.

One success followed another and Pullman soon became a millionaire. Changes, however, gradually brought misfortune, beginning in 1894 when Pullman, at the onset of a depression, suddenly reduced his employees' wages by 25%, and at the same time maintained the rent level for all his workers homes.

The employees reacted by going out on strike on May 11th and they got the support of the American Railroad Union. The strike spread over America and the great Pullman strike was a fact. To be sure, the trains began to roll again by July 20th, but under military protection.

The continuing misfortune brought down G. M. Pullman and may have contributed to his death on October 19, 1897, three years after the strike. In memory of those days the Chicago Federation of Labor organized a big parade on Labor Day, September 5th, 1994, in Pullman.

Many countries in Europe have manufactured Pullman cars for a long time and many others have followed his designs. On Sweden's part, there are examples in G. Nothin's *Carriage Science,* 1912, J. W. Fischerström's *Swedens' Railroads,* 1971, and in B. Kullander's *History of Sweden's Railroads,* 1994. They are woven together with Swedish railroad history and with the well-known years of the past; 1862, when the western main line was inaugurated; 1864, when the south main line was opened; 1872, when the possibility of lying down was instituted in first class by unfolding the seats; 1877, when the first bogie wheel systems were put into use; 1879, when the cars first used aisle passages; 1881, when gas lighting was introduced; 1883, when air brakes were installed; and 1897, when the first dining cars were placed in service.

Swedish Railway's very first order, however, was to be with Lauenstein & Co. in Hamburg as early as 1856, and Kockums began its production in 1861. Other big producers were Gothenburg's machine factory, Atlas Works in Stockholm, and Swedish Railroad Factories in Linköping, among others.

Innovations and changes in construction will be examined more closely in a coming section.

How and when did these changes reach Sweden and what transformed them in practice? There are still a few questions we must try to answer.

A summation of impressions so far, is that G. M. Pullman was an extremely remarkable man, a genius who, without any great education, not only started with a number of original ideas but also developed them, arranged backing for his expenses and risk capital, arranged patents, started mass production of his innovations, hired people, caused factories to be built, caused houses to be built, yes, a complete ideal town for not less than approximately 10,000 men.

He is regarded as one of the world's most creative entrepreneurs, and his innovations have spread over the world. Even if his own power came to a sudden end, its results have continued to our day. And even if the industries he created have been brought down, many of the buildings in the town of Pullman are still standing. Some of the public buildings are undergoing renovation, and are protected by The Illinois Historic Preservation Agency.

The company, however, was divided into three parts.

> 1. The Pullman Standard Car Manufacturing Co. continued to make sleeping cars; also freight cars, streetcars, and later, complete diesel streamlined trains for railroads such as The Union Pacific and the Illinois Central. They built freight cars in Bessemer, Alabama and Hammond, Indiana.
>
> 2. The Pullman Company owned and operated the sleeping cars in the usual way, and maintained them at their shops in Pullman.
>
> 3. Pullman Incorporated was a holding company, the executive branch that owned controlling stock in the other two. The corporate offices of the three companies remained in the Pullman Building in downtown Chicago. It was built at the same time as the town and Beman was also its architect.
>
> Raymond E. Johnson
> in a letter to the author
> 04/30/1996

In continuing, I pose questions about why Swedes came to the town of Pullman, how they conducted their lives and in what manner their culture was preserved.

I have drawn the theme of my work from Woodrow W. Eisenhart. He worked at Pullman Standard Car Manufacturing Company for 40 years, from 1937 to 1977.

He writes the following: "The Swedes were master craftsmen and became the manufacturing backbone of the company for many years to come, both in engineering and production in the shops." Eisenhart informed me in 1996, that he enjoyed every minute of his time with this great corporation and was proud of the manufactured product.

Besides my contact with Woodrow W. Eisenhart through the Vasa Order of America, Local lodge Siljan-Mora Tuna number 134, I have obtained abundant information from Raymond Johnson of Wheaton, Illinois. He holds the foremost place among my informants concerning Pullman.

Raymond E. Johnson's grandfather [father's father], Nils Gustaf Johannesson, was born in Grimeton parish, Halland on the torp, Pukasten in the year 1862, and worked in Göteborg until he emigrated to Chicago in 1884. There he found work as a carpenter at Pullman. In 1889 he married Frida Selin from Farstorp in Skåne. They rented a home at 734 Erikson, now 10514 Maryland, one of Pullman's row houses for his workers. They had six children who all began to work at Pullman as soon as they grew up. Raymond's father, Gustaf J. Johnson was born in 1889. He was advanced to "pattern maker" at Pullman. Raymond Johnson also began his career at Pullman. Later he became a teacher and author. In "A Search For Symmetry, Poems," Wheaton, 1996, 53 pages, he depicts, among other things, his time of growing up in Pullman and in the adjoining Roseland. Here I quote some lines from page 26.

> The immigrant workers of the Pullman shops play soccer. Swedish, Irish, Scots, Polish, Croats, Serbs, Slovaks, Germans. The play is intense and brutal, with ethnic hatreds brought over from the old country. The spectators are all men; they wear suits and neckties under heavy overcoats; wear felt fedora hats and smoke cigars.

It was thanks to my newspaper ads during the spring of 1995 that I received many good answers and the impetus to continue.

They confirmed my first observation that many skilled carpenters at Pullman had come from Sweden.

Among some 30 incoming answers, came one of particularly great interest, a collection of letters that Tage Åkerberg of Anneberg had the kindness to place at my disposition. His uncle [father's brother], Ernst (Ernest) Åkerberg over many years wrote home to his parents from his home in Pullman of his work as a carpenter at Pullman, and it is these letters which I was privileged to study.

Ernst Åkerberg had the company of at least 40 people from Nykyrke parish in the southeast part of Skaraborgs land. They came mostly from these farms: Alunda, Bosebygt, Bredared, Bråared, Ersered, Granbäck, Gunnarsbo, Halvstenshult, Hultet, Lilla Gålleryd, Mullsjö, Ryfors, Sörarp, and Sörarps Mill. The Åkerbergs came from Ersered. Most of these emigrants had their origin in the region around Mullsjö. The biggest family was the Hellströms from Sörarps Mill with no less than 10 emigrants during the time, 1881-1906. One of them, Pontus Hellström, returned in 1903.

During the years 1862-1863 Nykyrke parish received a railroad connection with Falköping and Jönköping, which brought about a new community culture centered around Mullsjö station. The bordering parish, Sandhem, also shows large emigration figures. As a rule, most of the families who moved from Nykyrke parish were property owners. The construction of the railroad tended to open these regions.

To connect again with the Chicago area, Anita Ruth Olson characterizes the Swedes in the same way in her "Conclusion," 1990, page 293 ff. It comes at the end of her doctors dissertation, and I have found it to be a well-founded assessment of the situation for Swedes in Chicago from 1880 to 1920:

> Swedish immigrants who arrived and lived in Chicago between 1880 and 1920 found that the social, economic, and geographic environment compared with their experience in Sweden.

Even if nationalism was strong in Sweden, the Swedes evidently became, in many ways, more self confident in the American environment than many of them had been in the homeland. Studies show how Swedes adapted to city life, how immigrant groups formed the outlines of an American city, and how they manifested their presence there.

The official statistics show that there were 1,024 Swedish workers at Pullman in 1885, constituting 11.9%. Americans placed first with 4,013 (46.6%), Germans second with 1,088 (12.6%), Irish fourth (6.5%) and so forth.

The Purpose

The purpose of my work is to show a noticeable *chosen part* of the town's and the industry's histories, and specifically that of the Swedish carpenters.

The main questions which are raised, and in turn will be answered in their context, are these:

Why was the Pullman town built, how was it built, what innovative car technology originated at Pullman, why did Swedes come to the town of Pullman, how did their daily lives function, and in what way was their culture created?

The history of the immigrants from Ryfors runs like a red thread through the work.

Considerations of method

The research environment at the Nordic Museum was crucial to my work, as it was to the training of numerous colleagues who emerged from it. Ever since Sigurd Erixon's and Sigfrid Svensson's culture seminars, the science studies have been important to me. During my years as head of the museum in Gothenburg and also thereafter, I have had the advantage of attending Sven B. Ek's research seminars with their underlying insights into the everyday man.

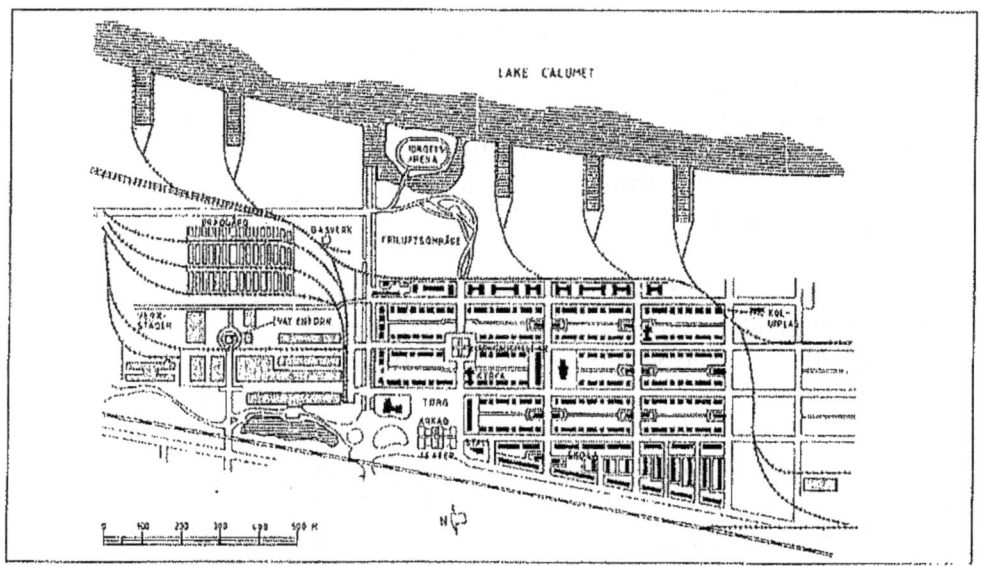

Map of Pullman by Anhlund Brunnstrom. Identified in Swedish are: lumber yard, gas plant, shops, water tower, market hall, church, plaza, arcade, theater, school, coal yard, sports arena, leisure area.

An early Pullman car which could be converted to a sleeping car. The upper bed panels are richly decorated. When the beds are not in use they are folded up to the ceiling. From Encyclopedia of Railways, *1968, p. 228.*

Chapter II
Swedes Who Lived And Worked In Pullman
My Inquiry

Advertisements and Replies

My "advertising" was done in April 1995. It was introduced in the week of the 16th in *The Worker, The Bohuslander, Jönköping-Post, New Värmland Times, Skaraborg Land Times,* and *Svenska Dagbladet.* In addition it was introduced in the magazines *The Bridge* and *Swedish Contact,* and it stated the following:

Pullman in Chicago

Perhaps you know someone who worked there? It was common knowledge in Chicago during the decades around the turn of the century 1900, that carpenters at Pullman had come from Sweden. All railway cars, sleeping cars with folding upper beds, and unsurpassed dining cars were manufactured at Pullman. The workers lived in the town of Pullman, a model town also planned by the founder and owner, George Mortimer Pullman.

About 10,000 workers lived in Pullman when it flourished at its best. However, in 1894 he felt himself called upon to lower his employees' wages because of an impending depression. It was then that the well-known Pullman strike broke out on May 11, and after the strike the great Pullman Company never completely recovered. But the worst was over by September 5th. In 1994, the 100th anniversary, a great parade was organized that began at the corner of 111th Street and Cottage Grove Avenue in Chicago.

In connection with the above I wondered if the newspapers would be willing to help me make contact with some of the Pullman workers who had returned, and also their families.

Here is a sampling of the answers I received: The informants have given me permission to use their names and addresses.

Axel Ekfeldt, Tullgatan 2, Eskilstuna, wrote on 04/27/1995 as follows:

Your inquiry in today's *Svenska Dagbladet* about Swedes employed at Pullman in Chicago awakens childhood memories both happy and sad. What I knew about the shareholder family Albin Andersson in Vassbotten bay at Lake Vänern was that the Anderssons emigrated to USA and worked in the Pullman factory in Chicago, which we boys were quite impressed with. At a guess, the family returned home in the middle of the 1920 decade. In Naglum's churchyard rest the remains of Albin (died 1934) and Matilda Andersson. Naturally we boys were impressed that they both lived for many years in the big land in the west and particularly that they made Pullman cars. I know that the family brought back from USA a wealth of experience. This should help your detective work.

Arvid Gustavsson, Rönngatan 14, Mullsjö:

Had an uncle, Richard Fröjd, a young fellow who worked at Pullman. I believe he was a carpenter. The photo is in the family. 08/05/95

Martin Karlsson, Ödest

My father, Oscar Karlsson worked at a factory in Illinois that made undercarriages for Pullman cars. He was also at Pullman on a number of occasions. 05/08/1995

Erik Lindh, Österbymo;

I knew a man who became a supervisor at Pullman and had a collection of 100 letters to Sweden. 05/08/1995

Marianne Salborn, Furugatan 6, Norrahammar:

My father, Axel Gardell and an uncle, Per Gardell, born 1878, and an uncle, August Brandt, worked at Pullman. Per and August remained in America. 05/08/1995

James E. Stone, 672 Huntington Drive, Bowling Green Kentucky introduced his letter of 06/02/1996 in this way: [In English]

A family friend has sent me a copy of *The Bridge* in which information about Pullman Works is being sought.

I am first generation American whose parents arrived from Sweden in the 1920s. My mother came from Falun in Kopparberg and my father from Kristinehamn in Värmland. Both my father and his brother worked for the Pullman Company. Their father was K. August Olson of Kräggeshyttan. In explanation of the name change, I was told that my grandfather's brothers had been in the Swedish Army and had gotten the "army names" of Sten. When my father and his siblings went to school they had the same schoolmaster as grandfather. This schoolmaster knew of the army name and used Sten "unge" [young ones] as names for the children when they started in school. In any event when Dad emigrated to America he entered as Victor Emil Sten and his brother as J. Henrik Sten. This was later changed to Stone for both of them.

Dad was born March 22, 1901, and my uncle Henry was born in the late 1890s. Both worked at Pullman. Dad arrived in July or August 1920 and worked at Pullman in the mid to late 1920s and again for a one-year period during the U.S. depression sometime between 1932 and 1937. Henry worked continuously for Pullman until sometime in the early 1950s before returning to Sweden where he died of cancer.

Somewhere in the family papers I may have more specific information, but I hope this will be helpful in your search.

Grete Nyström, Hägerstensvägen, 161, Hägersten, 06/22/1995

I read in *Svenska Dagbladet* your advertisement for Swedes who worked at Pullman. I had an uncle who worked there. My grandmother and grandfather emigrated to USA in the early 1860s. Good friends wrote that they had a big farm. Grandmother was extremely unhappy; she would have been better off in Sweden. My mother was born in Pennsylvania. The family moved to Chicago where grandfather had a business. He was robbed and beaten so badly that he became blind. They were advised by the family to seek help in Sweden. Three of the children returned to USA with good work training. The son Ernst Sahlberg was trained as a carpenter and was also a draftsman. According to my mother they were employed at Pullman. In the 1930s depression he returned to Sweden and took up residence in Visnums Parish.

Lilly Sundell, Fiskebäckskil, June, 1995:

I read your ad in the *Bohuslander*. I know Oskar Sundell's name. I was married to his son Gustav who passed away a year ago. Oskar traveled to America when Gustav, who was the youngest of eight children, was three years old. Later one of Oscar's sons, Carl, also came to America. He continued to live there 87 years. He had been in Sweden several times. I heard through his siblings that they both had the same work in America at Pullman.

Bud Larsson, 64 Avalon Blvd. Jamestown, NY. 02/25/1996 [In English]

Carl Otto Lundgren, 1854-1935, worked for Pullman as a carpenter and cabinet maker. He was born in Skåne. He got a job with the Swedish railroad. He decided to go to Australia as there was no work for him anymore on the railroad. When at the boat depot he saw a sign on the wall saying: "George Pullman hiring carpenters to build his cars." He bought his ticket and came to the USA. Got a job with Pullman car. I believe it might have been in Buffalo, N.Y. because 3 more children were born there. He then came to Jamestown N.Y. and was a carpenter.

Bertil G. Winström, Bishop Hill, IL 61419, 02/07/1996 [In English]

I noticed in the last issue of *The Bridge* that you are interested in persons who worked for the Pullman Co.

My cousin, Eric Pihl, worked for Pullman until he retired and moved to California.

Eric was born in Nykroppa, Värmland. Eric's father and my mother were siblings.

I saw in the Bessemer #203 [a lodge] obituaries that Eric died a couple of years ago. I do not know if Eric's wife Hanna is still living. Their latest address was or is 330 W. Highway 246, Space 106, Buellton, Cal. 93427.

Hanna operated the Hotel Pullman and restaurant until they retired.

I am sure that Woodrow Eisenhart can check on Eric and Hanna by looking up their records in the Bessemer #203. I presume that they originally belonged to Roseland #128 where most of the Pullman people belonged.

Commentary

This is the place to comment on the answers to the advertisements. They show that there continues to be a considerable number of Swedes who knew Pullman. The answers gave suggestions for contacting sources through which I got newspaper clippings, photos, and much more. It was thanks to these that during continuing contacts I made use of such Pullman sources as Josef Bergström from Sunne, Henry Nordlund from Östra Ämtervik, David E. Nordqvist from Västra Ämtervik, Ture Carlsson from Kalvön in Fjällbacka, Eric Nordstrand from Hunnebostrand, Harry Norlin from Munkedal, Oscar Sundell from Kville, Folke F. Persson from Lidköping, and Carl Ström from Tidaholm. Earlier I had information about emigrants from Kristinehamn, Nykroppa, Visnum, Vassbotten, Fiskebäckskil, Mullsjö, Norrahammar, and Gränna, which could be interpreted as a recruiting region with extensions from Värmland, Bohuslän, Västergötland, and North Småland.

Two individual destinies, part of a greater connection

Åkerberg

Tage Åkerberg had seen the appeal in *Jönköpings-Post*, 04/20/1995 and informed me of his letter collection which he generously placed at my disposition. The letters that his uncle Ernst (Ernest) Åkerberg wrote home to his parents from the town of Pullman, I will now present in this section.

On 09/14/1902 Ernst wrote to his parents from Axvall that he had just been up to see Captain Kuylenstierna and had shown his certificate. One of his documents, however, had not the wording it should have had. Therefore he asked that his parents go to the parish registrar's office and get a new one. The wording should have been as follows:

That the bearer 65 79/01 Ernst Hjalmar Åkerberg who intends to emigrate to North Americas United States has at his disposition a capital of three hundred Kronor, validated hereby on the requested certificate. Nykyrka Mullsjö etc.

The next letter is dated Göteborg [Gothenburg] 11/18/1902. Ernst reports then, that he is well and happy. He has bought the ticket. The next day he will go to the police office to have his papers examined and then finally go to the boat at mid-day. There are likely to be many passengers boarding the same boat. Göteborg is a little different than Jönköping, he writes; the streetcars go fast and the steamboats in the harbor are frightfully big. Next time the parents will learn how he fared on the North Sea.

"Next time" was 12/04/1902 from Pullman, and it was a very difficult journey. The ship had left Liverpool on 11/22 and arrived in Boston first on 12/01. The waves were as high "as the ladugården at home." "One had to lie and hold on with both hands to avoid being washed into the waves." A woman from Ireland died and was buried at sea. "They read the same service as at a grave. The captain did it."

The trip to Chicago took them through Buffalo. In Pullman Åkerberg was promptly taken to meet Nykyrke neighbors. He lived and ate with Karl and August Hurtig, and Fritiof (Hillstrom) promised "to speak for him" at Pullman. He seemed to be happy right away, for on 12/10 he bought new shoes, a new hat and other things, "all more durable and cheaper than in Sweden." More permanently on 12/29 he began the work he called "stripping." It consisted of repairing windows and doors in railway cars.

01/10/1903 He reported that Christmas had been pleasant. At the Hillströms they had the evening meal on Christmas Eve with dip in the bowl[1] and Lutfisk. Those who were missed were spoken of, and he particularly missed Ida and his little brother, John.

01/27/1903 he described his workday, which began at 6:30 with breakfast, and then no break before 12:00 with one hour lunch. But there was no possibility of sleeping for a while at mid-day as they did at home. Work stopped for the day at 6:00 except on Saturdays, when they were free at 1:00. Then he was glad to travel in to Chicago and meet "Norlings boys." They traveled through Chicago in the new streetcars. "We rode in the air, for here they have railways that go above the houses; they are frightening. Yes, it is indeed pleasant to come out in the world and get to see a little more than Ryfors." He was eager to show further that it only cost 15 cents for the distance Pullman-Chicago and still it was equivalent to the distance Mullsjö-Jönköping. The stated desire this time was that his parents should buy "Vademecum"[2] for him and send it with "Sandstedt's brother."

In his letter of 02/25/1903 he writes that he now has a better work assignment; to place the rubber strip on the windows and doors. "We are six who do this work," and the Pullman parlor cars made the strongest impression on him along with the dining cars. "Well, I just can't express how fine they are."

Chicago's highest building with 23 floors had also impressed him. "One looks down from it and sees people looking just like ants, and I cannot understand how they can build them so frighteningly high."

On 03/22/1903 he had noticed the first tokens of spring, the grass was becoming green and the bushes were budding: "It is beautiful when summer approaches, as long as one has his health, and one has work. I like mine very much, and the pay isn't so bad either with 20 cents an hour. "So I look after myself very well." He notes that his monthly expenses amount to 15 dollars for food and only 3 for the room. He expresses admiration at this time for the value of the switching system of the railroads; "They don't need to run around and change for every train as they do in Sweden."

03/31/1903 He was pleased with a notice that Pullman would introduce a 9 hour workday instead of 10, "but we will have the same pay in any case so that is really good." Should it not go through, he feared there would be a strike. "You will reflect that there are at least 10,000 workers at Pullman, so it doesn't do for the company to make a fuss."

05/02/1903 He reports, in part, that on Wednesday evening he had been to a wedding with "August and Karl." It was a Swedish boy, Karl Jansson, who was married in the Swedish church in Pullman. A few hundred were invited to the evening meal afterwards in the church's basement. There were many presents; by the youth society, a dining room table and four chairs. They cost 40 dollars, so they were very fine. And in part, he reported that he had moved from number 320 to 340 on the same street. Also he was now lodging with Swedes, "just as nice as the others." Both his friends moved with him but now they rented two rooms instead of one. In addition, he had been in Chicago again and bought a very handsome suit, and a pair of shoes for three dollars, and this thanks to his now making 24 ½ cents per hour.

In his letter of 07/17/1903 he gives an example of how severe the summer heat was. He was so exhausted when he came home after work that he only wanted to sleep and was not in the mood to write, but anyway, now he must report that he had a new job at Pullman, "It is called trimming; we put in all the fittings in the cars so now I have become a full carpenter, but I am really not as skilled as the older carpenters."

Fritiof Hillstrom does the same work, and I have him to thank for it, "that I am where I am now, for he helped me from the very beginning."

One night this week he worked overtime, but what happiness when he came home! "Four letters waited for me, one from Ida, one from Mia, one from Helena and one from Modig. It was so great."

In August he earned 35 dollars in 14 days, 08/31/1903, and with the laundry it is now very nice. "Every Monday I can lay out everything I want washed. Then it comes back clean and folded one day a week."

09/28/1903 He had been to Chicago and equipped himself for 19 dollars. "Here with hardly a weeks pay one can clothe himself from top to toe. On that subject, I have bought myself the tools I need for almost 20 dollars. We do very fine work here so one must have a little of everything. I am not so clumsy a carpenter as you may think." He hadn't arrived yet. It can very likely take a few years before he can do everything, and he thought he could manage his trouble with English. Pullman has a night school. "Well, everything is possible if one wills it."

10/07/1903 He begins as usual with "Beloved parents" and inquires how they are and that he is well. The letter continues with thanks for the stockings which the family had sent him, "It shows that mamma thinks of me even if I am so far away." Then he relates that he and Fritiof have been going out on Saturdays to meet Helena. She had been living with her sister, Hulda in Jamestown, NY. On Sunday he was home with Swedish friends and at supper. "We talked about everything possible from old Ryfors. It is no wonder that Filip wants to leave Ryfors, for there is really no future there and I never regret that I left."

11/08/1903 He tells that he has moved again. Now to Fritiof Hillstrom, who had a room to rent. "I have often had both food and coffee with them, but it would be so much nicer if Robert were also here in Pullman and had a job. Helena is also here now and has a place already. I will go tomorrow to visit her."

12/10 is the last letter dated 1903. He thought naturally enough, that it would be nice to come home and dip in the bowl, but "the distance is too great." He had great pleasure in sending Christmas presents to his parents and to his little brother. He also sends his greetings to Ida and to Mia Sandstedt and thanks for the Christmas presents he received, among others, the good ginger cookies. These he got through Filip, the eighth and last of Karl Alfred Hellström's sons, who left Sweden for America. All is written with good hopes, but the message that Ida at home had been married had made him dismayed and sad.

The first letter of the year 1904 is dated the day after New Years Day. Ernest Åkerberg, as he now called himself, first wished all at home a happy New Year and writes that he didn't know anything about Christmas Day. He didn't even celebrate Boxing Day [next day] except to go directly to work, that is, overtime. It was cold and snowy every day. This, his second Christmas in Pullman had evidently not been as pleasant as the first. "I hardly know what to write because I haven't been anywhere the whole Christmas."

01/16/1904 He writes of Ida, his sister, and of her marriage to Arvid. "Well, it was disturbing that it was such a quick decision. I think it was strange that Ida didn't let me hear anything about it. I would more than gladly give Ida a wedding present, but when I didn't get to know until afterwards, I don't think I can do that. But greet Ida from me and wish her happiness and prosperity in her marriage."

Soon he had recovered his mood again and had welcomed and been to the homes of the two families from Nykyrke, Reinhold and Johan Hillström. "We had such fun and Helena was also there of course. She didn't think much of her first place so she left there. Here one can come one day and go the next. Helena asks me to send a particular greeting to Mamma and to Ida."

02/23/1904 He was happy that a letter had just arrived from home. "Happy to hear that you all are well and feel good. Here in Pullman everything is going smoothly and we have constant work. Yes, it is strange that the work can stretch out for those who do so terribly much work as we have this year. There are nearly 9000 workers and when one thinks of how much they can accomplish in one day..."

"Now they are starting to build 'luxury cars' that will go to the big summer Worlds Fair in St. Louis, exceptionally beautiful cars with genuine gold plated fittings and hinges. I wish you could see one of them."

February they got their wages, or "Peda" as they called it, 35 dollars, 47 cents for 14 days, and such a wage he had never had in "Old Ryfors."

At the end of the letter he sent greetings from all the Hellstroms, particularly from Fritiof and his wife with whom he had lived and, as a postscript, "from (my) girl Helena." "It takes one hour by streetcar for her to come out to Pullman from her place," he added this information for his parents.

04/11/1904 He confirmed that those cars had gone to the St. Louis Fair. They must have cost over a million dollars. He was proud of them, and that he knew different details and phases were his work, and that it goes very well with the language now. He earned all of 44 dollars and 29 cents, but "Old Ryfors always comes first in their conversations" when he meets Fritiof and Helena sometimes in the evenings.

05/22/1904 It was full summer and as beautiful as one could wish. He had been to church and met many acquaintances, many "from Ryfors" who had sent greetings. The Fritiofs, his landlords, had, by the way, "had a little girl." He met the Hurtig boys almost every day at work, and they lived only a few minutes away from each other, and so close he can go over and talk to them. And he wondered "why Ida never writes to Helena," and closes by saying he would also like to have a letter from his little brother, John, and puts a dollar in his letter for him.

07/23/1904 He sat down to write immediately after coming home from working a half day at the shop. It had been hot as an oven for a long time. Now, however a worry had emerged because they had become short of work at Pullman. "Several hundred have had notice for awhile, but we trimmers haven't heard anything yet." He is still taking it calmly "for I have, as they say, a little at the bottom of the chest."

09/26/1904. Now he himself had been temporarily dismissed until further notice and had been out of work for 14 days, and "The time goes slowly when one has nothing to do, but we can have fun anyway because there are so many Ryfors people here at Pullman and we visit one another every day."

"Karl and August have gone to see the fair at St. Louis. Myself, I have gone with another Swede to visit Chicago's big stockyards. Every day they butcher 25,000 animals. They are cut up and prepared in not more than three minutes." To pass the time he had begun to buy wood to do some carpentry. The bright spots are the times in the week when he can visit Helena.

11/28/1904 is the last dated letter and like those he wrote in Pullman earlier, opens with, "Beloved parents, I hope you are well" and ends with loving greetings "signed Ernest Åkerberg" and with thanks for the gifts which came "with Severin" when he returned from Sweden. They consisted of cookies and cigars.

But two months had gone by since he had worked at Pullman and the shop had been closed. "After New Years, however, they believe that it will go ahead again." Occasional work in another department on freight cars earning three dollars a day had helped keep up the funds but it "was hard" and the new job had given him pain in the hands. In the evenings he began to go to school again between 7 and 9, to read and write, "...and sometimes we even sang." It cost nearly nothing, "...ink and pen and paper we got free so it was really foolish to sleep away the time."

After following Ernest Åkerberg through his letters for two years now, the question presents itself of how it went afterwards. Tage Åkerberg answered my question in this way: Ernest Hjalmar Åkerberg who was born in 1880, married "his girl" Helena, born Hellström. She had 10 siblings. All emigrated to America. Ernst and Helena revisited Sweden once. Helena first in 1906 when she also brought her father over to be present at Ernst and Helena's wedding the same year. Ernst went back in 1912 with his eldest son, Arnold.

He died in 1954 and his brother who in the letters was called "little John" was Tage Åkerberg's father. John was born in 1895 and worked there as a blacksmith until his death in 1951. Their parents were Carl Johan Åkerberg (1844-1930) and Emma Sofia born Hurtig (1853-1934). The grandfather came to Ryfors factory outside Mullsjö in 1867 and had a position as supervisor. The grandmother was born in Ryfors, where her father was a binder.

We will continue to follow Ernest Åkerberg and his family in Chapter 8, but now to my most important informant.

Johnson:

From my other flowing source, Raymond E. Johnson and the letter exchanges with him, I now continue this chapter. Raymond E. Johnson tells mostly of his mother's parents, Gustaf Adolph Johansson (1860-1929) and Anna Josefina Hedberg Johansson (1862-1955).

Gustaf Adolph Johansson grew up on the farm, Dalen in Naglums parish, Älvsborgs land. His parents were Johan Andersson and Britta Maria Hansdotter who were from Vänersnäs and Ale-Skövde respectively. Gustaf emigrated to Chicago in 1881 with his brother, Carl Herman, who was two years older. "Their destination was Pullman," where they both found work. "Gustaf sent for Anna in 1882. They were married in 1883. Carl Herman met his wife in Pullman. They both bought homes on 111th Place in the adjoining community of Roseland and raised their families there." Anna came from Foss parish in Bohuslän. Her parents were Johannes Hedberg and Helena Hansdotter. When Anna was born her parents lived in Valbo-Ryr, Dalsland. Her older brother, Alexander Stefanus, also emigrated to America the same year as Anna but not on the same boat. Their sister, Maria, also came five years later. Only Anna remained in Chicago.

Raymond asked her to tell of her arrival at Chicago in 1882, and the record he made reads as follows: [in English]

"I once asked her about her arrival and her experience with immigration processing. She said it was confusing and frightening. The immigration terminal was in Brooklyn then; Ellis Island was not opened until 1892. When her train arrived in Chicago Gustaf was waiting for her at the 63rd Street station but Anna didn't know she was to get off there and rode to the terminal in the Loop. Gustaf guessed what had happened and made his way downtown as quickly as possible. Meanwhile Anna, not knowing any English or where she was, just sat and waited. It was another frightening experience followed by a joyful reunion."

Anna and Gustaf were married on March 13, 1883 in the Cook County Building. Gustaf and his brother, Carl Herman worked as axle turners at Pullman and lived in homes near lake Calumet at 117th Street, the area just south of Pullman town known as the brickyard. The Pullman Company made their own bricks there.

"The town of Pullman and the car shops were quite new then and thousands of immigrants from many countries were employed there. The town was laid out in row-houses resembling European cities. Carl Herman met his wife in the brickyard neighborhood. She was Ingrid Carolina Nelson, who was known to us ever after as Faster Ida. [pronounced Foster]."

Of his father Gust J. Johnson and his uncle [mother's brother] Hjalmar, Raymond writes as follows:

"My father was a pattern maker, (as I am sure you know, machine parts were metal castings made in sand molds, and wood patterns were used to make the impressions in the sand). His father was a molder in the foundries at Pullman and with many other manufacturers around South Chicago. It is my impression that both of these crafts enjoyed great prestige among the workers of the time. This may partly answer your question about how workers felt about their work."

"During the Depression (early 1930s) when jobs were hard to find, my father found temporary work at Pullman, where they were making a special luxury lounge car for exhibit at the Chicago World's Fair of 1933-1934. It had ornamental paneling in the Art Deco style made of cast aluminum and he made some of the patterns for it. He showed us with pride the parts he had made when we visited the car at the fair." Letter to the author 06/03/96

"My Uncle Hjalmar was born in 1884 and remembered the strike of 1894. He told me of the soldiers in the streets and the tension everyone felt. After the strike the company was ordered to sell the houses to the workers, which they did in 1907. Many of the workers had preferred to buy houses in nearby Roseland. My grandparents did so in about 1890. When I was growing up there the water tower and clock tower were constant visible landmarks. I think the history in the material I enclose will answer most of the questions you ask in your letter. I don't think anyone knows how many Scandinavians Pullman employed—there were many, but also [in my time] many Italians, Irish, Scots, Polish, Lithuanians, Slovaks, Czechs. There must have been women in clerical jobs. You will notice the Pullman Bank was optimistic about the community's future in 1958, but unfortunately it did not turn out that way. Lake Calumet was developed as a port for international shipping, but the communities of Chicago's South Side have fallen to decay and high crime rate. The former residents have moved to the suburbs."

"I hope I am not presumptuous in including my poem about Farfars Mor, Severina. [grandfather's mother]. It is extracted from my biography of her. She was born Feb. 7, 1832 in Rolfstorp parish,

Hallands land. The poem poses the question, 'Why did they come?' and this was my quest in all my research."

"It has been great fun for me to gather this material and I hope it will be of some use to you. If there are more questions, don't hesitate to ask—I would be most happy to help."

"...the grave of my great-grandmother, Severina Jönsdotter. How Severina came to rest in this beautiful place [Springvale cemetery, Lafayette, IN] so remote and different from the place of her birth, is a fascinating story; one that might be held typical of the millions who left the lands of their birth; who made their hazardous journeys to an unknown land and an unpredictable future. In her story we may find an answer to the question—why did they come"?

Letter to the author 04/30/96

"Pigan" [the servant girl] Severina Jönsdotter was born at the torp Ugglarp #3 in Rolfstorp. She married Johannes Andreasson in 1854. They lived on Hukeretorp [tenant holding] on the farm Thorstorp in Grimeton parish. Their children, Anders Samuel and Johan Algot were born in 1857 and 1859 respectively. Johannes is registered there as a laborer. Raymond E. Johnson's Grandfather [father's father] Nils Gustaf Johannesson was born, as already mentioned, on June 6, 1862.

Johannes died on November 5, 1870. Johan Algot emigrated first to Boston, then to Chicago. He became a politician and building contracter in Lafayette IN. He died in Oklahoma City in 1913. It was said of him that "He was a man of rugged character and his integrity was never questioned." Algot financed Nils Gustaf's trip overseas. He came and established himself as a foundry worker at Pullman.

His oldest child was Raymond's father. Nils Gustaf told of "How desperately poor they had been, and how wonderful it was to live in the United States." Nils Gustaf's brother, Carl Otto, also worked in Chicago but later moved to Lafayette, Indiana, where he became fire chief. He died in 1934.

Severina "left for America in 1888." Of her travels in America Raymond writes:

"When we think of a seventy-year-old woman traveling alone on the railroads at the turn of the century on a regular round of Chicago, Lafayette, Oklahoma City, and Seattle we may gather that she was well endowed with endurance and spirit."

"Like many people from the old country she was frightened of thunderstorms. When they happened each sentence of her prayers began with, Käre Gud. She never did learn English, partly because she did not need to, all her children and grandchildren spoke Swedish. She was a tiny woman, full of energy and extremely gregarious."

Raymond concludes his story of her with a poem in which he is fascinated with her name and her destiny. It is titled "Severina" and I cite some of the lines in it, written in October, 1986, published in *Rivulets V,* 1993, p. 1 ff.

> And out of that darkness came Severina Jönsdotter, age nineteen.
> Now with a surname—given by whom?
> A sympathetic priest? A family who loved her? Only she knew.
> > *Severina, cute and prim*
> > *did you know your father's name?*
> > *or who gave you your patronym*
> > *as sanctuary from your shame?*
> She married a farmhand.
> Piga and dräng,[3] they faced life together in village and torp.
> Then widowed by the lung sickness.
> Left alone with five small children.
> Tried to feed them, living in a stuga—
> a widows' cabin, ward of the parish.
> When the priest made his call
> the boys cried in protest as he accepted the proffered coffee
> and ate tomorrow's food.
> And the scolded boys were sent to bed.
> And the growing boys soon left the farm
> and went to the city to work;
> to pool their money to go to Amerika.
> They sent for their mother
> when they found the means.
> And she found herself, for the first time in her life
> in a caring, benevolent community,
> where she watched her sons prosper;
> become leaders and builders
> of university buildings;
> a land where her sons had opportunity
> limited only by their own abilities.
> She traveled alone across the wide country
> to live for a time with one of her children
> and then move on to the next;
> restless, curious, gregarious, vital.

Raymond E. Johnson,
"Severina 1832-1912"
in *Rivulets V,* 1993, page 1ff

One cannot escape feeling strongly for Severina Jönsdotter, who died on February 27, 1912 in Lafayette, Indiana in the home of her son, Carl Otto.

In 1889, Raymond's mother's parents, Gustaf and Anna bought a little house of their own in Roseland, the neighboring community to Pullman, at 15 W 111th Place. Carl Herman and his family lived in the next block near Wentworth Avenue. The two families were very close. Anna became the "matriarch" of the large Johnson family in Roseland.

In 1883 Anna and Gustaf belonged to a little group of Swedes who wanted to build a Swedish Lutheran church in this region. They first rented a room in the Pullman Arcade building. But the congregation did not hesitate long [1885] before building their own church, and it was at the corner of 113th street and Forest Avenue. It was named, as we know, Elim Church. The children used the

Swedish bible and they were taught the difference between right and wrong. Raymond relates further, that Anna was convinced "...that everyone will surely speak Swedish in heaven, because she didn't see how people could really communicate otherwise."

Anna volunteered to help in a women's auxiliary organization of the church, the Sofia society. Raymond remembers that he always associated the smell of coffee with his grandmother and with the atmosphere in her home.

"I always associate the smell of brewing coffee with Grandma. The same Swedish atmosphere prevailed in the home of her sister-in-law, Faster, where Mother's cousins lived. I can remember all the Swedish ladies seated around the table with a freshly-ironed table cloth on it. They would place a piece of lump sugar under their tongues while they sipped their coffee with real, thick cream in it. There was plenty of coffee cake and butter too. No wonder most of them were heavy. They all seemed to be talking at once, always in Swedish. Grandma only spoke English when she had to. I recall a conversation she had in Bangor, Michigan—her summer home—with a lady from the church who had come for coffee. She told of her frustration at bible classes because nobody there understood Swedish and she could not express her deepest feelings in English. She once told me I should take pride in the fact that I was one hundred per-cent Swedish."

Anna also related some episodes from the Chicago World's Fair in 1893, and how she experienced life during the first and second world wars. In the foreground, of course, stood the family, with the old relatives in Sweden, the children and their families, and later the grandchildrens' achievements and their devastation during the Second World War.

Anna Johnson died at the age of 93. The funeral was held in Elim Church, and Raymond concluded his story of her in this way: "I served as pallbearer along with her other grandsons. She had requested that a hymn be sung, the favorite of her husband, Gustaf, *Tryggare kan ingen vara.*"

A large part of this family was tied to Pullman in Chicago as carpenters and molders and also lived in the town of Pullman. Elim Church and its pastors meant much to them, but some of them belonged to the Mission Church.

One branch of this family had come from Dalsland, another from Halland, and a third, the Selins, from Skåne.

"Mother used to tell me that Frida Selin, my grandmother who died before I was born, spoke in the Skånic accent, which, as a child, I was able to recognize as different from the other Swedish accents I was surrounded with in those days. Therefore I had some idea of what Frida's speech sounded like."

Raymond's mother, Lillian Johnson, was born in 1893 in Roseland. She had five siblings. The sisters were, during part of their lives, living and working at home, and her brother worked for many years at Pullman. His parents met each other at Palmer Park.

"They were married the following year, June 10, 1916. Just after Warren was born in 1919, they bought the home at 45 West 108th Place from Mother's cousins, Arthur and Sigurd Hedberg. This is where we boys grew up, and where Dad died in 1966. As a young couple they enjoyed a social life with their families and friends. From what I can remember their activities seemed typical of the Twenties decade. They had a car, a home, telephone, radio, and all the necessities within the reach of the workingman's income. Families did not scatter in those days; Mother was within reach and in constant touch with her brother and sisters; her mother and father lived just around the corner on State Street. Our big holidays were celebrated mostly with them."

Once when relatives of Raymond's grandparents came to visit unannounced they killed a hen or a few chickens who strutted about their little chicken coop, and from the garden dug up some new potatoes and vegetables to prepare a meal. Grandfather could also go hunting at the shores of Lake

Calumet. He liked to sing with his children at the end of a day's work and to accompany them on the little organ he bought. After they had sung he took down the bible. It was in Swedish. Gradually his children learned to read in it, but he had to explain many words to them. Because their father was so handy and versatile the children believed he could fix anything in the home. His children had few toys from the store, but they had books they could borrow from the school library. Next door neighbors at 15 West 111th Place were the families Sodergren on one side and the Anderssons on the other. Some in the families died in the 1918 Spanish influenza epidemic in Chicago.

Summary

A summary of this chapter shows that many Swedes were encouraged to travel to Chicago to find work at Pullman. The possibilities of finding work and housing were also good. The Pullman factory's reputation as an innovative enterprise was well-founded. The reputation of Pullman town certainly took a blow in connection with the Pullman strike in 1894, but it was in the 1930s depression when interest in finding work at Pullman first began to cool. Ernst Åkerberg's letters have given us an insight into how life could be shaped for a young Swedish carpenter in the beginning of the 20th century. His situation can surely be characterized as very favorable: He knew many people from the farms in Nykyrke parish in the southeast part of Skaraborgs land all the way from Alunda to Sörarp, and he was particularly known, as we have already seen, to the Hillström, Hurtig and Norling families. It was they who helped him find work and housing. They also invited him home for dinner now and then and showed him around in the surroundings, first in Pullman town with its Elim Church, its school and businesses, and soon also in Chicago, the big world-class city where everything aroused his astonishment: Streetcars that "dashed around on the streets," railway cars that "went above the houses," the great warehouses, the high skyscrapers and the big slaughterhouses. He was amazed at how they could build "so frighteningly high," and that they "slaughtered 25,000 animals per day" at the stockyards.

He expressed his surprise at how easy it was to go into Chicago and that it was so cheap to shop there. Shoes and clothes were of better quality than in Sweden. For only a weeks wages one could dress up from top to toe. "Well, it is certainly nice to come out into the world and get to see a little more than Ryfors," he wrote home. He liked the work and the salary wasn't bad. In 1903 a 9-hour workday was introduced instead of 10 hours, and this without decreasing the wages. As one of those 10,000 workers he was reasonably satisfied with his work assignment, particularly of course when he was promoted. "So now I have become a full carpenter" as he expressed it, "even if I don't feel that I am on a par with the old carpenters."

Contacts with his parents at home and with his siblings throughout this time was significant. How happy he was when he got mail! "Four letters were waiting for me," he exclaimed on one occasion. He looked forward to his evening lessons at Pullman School. He made progress there with his English, and the lessons were fun; "Sometimes we even sing."

He also told of Elim Church, where among other things, he was invited to a wedding in April, 1904, when Karl Janson was married. A few hundred were invited. A dinner was served in the church, and the youth society gave the bridal pair "some remarkably nice presents."

Elim Church also played an important role for the Johnson family in communion, baptism, confirmation, and burial. This family was likewise tied to the Pullman shops and the town of Pullman. Raymond E. Johnson's play with other children of immigrants remains as in a romantic glow throughout those years, as he writes in his book, "A Search For Symmetry."

In his first letter to me, April 9, 1996, Raymond writes of himself:

"I was born in 1920 in a part of Chicago known as Roseland, which is adjacent to the Pullman community. All of my grandparents were Swedish immigrants who came in the 1880s. My father was born in the town of Pullman. My grandfathers, my father, uncles, my brother, and countless neighbors, worked in the Pullman shops at one time or another. I grew up in the Roseland-Pullman community, and its streets and buildings have a 'home town' familiarity to me."

The big families and the many friends spread themselves gradually over the entire Chicago region, which became their home town: "The Loop, the Field Museum of Natural History, the beautiful lake front, Lincoln Park, Sports Café, Michigan Boulevard."

The celebration of Sweden Day at the big worlds fair, "The Columbian Exposition of 1893" was spoken of by many of the families, as were the Swedish singing societies, the gymnastic clubs, and the different provincial guilds. On the South Side was the Iduna Singing Club since 1885 and The North Star Singing Club since 1903; The Swedish-American Athletic Association since 1914, and IGOT Faithful since 1903.

All that Raymond related to me of his life and his family runs like a red thread through the next chapter devoted to the Elim congregation, but here I close my portrayal of these private individuals and their unique living standards. Those who, above all, give a human face to my story.

After my own studies in Pullman town and my going through the previously mentioned archive material, the results of which have been presented, I thought it would be interesting if I could make contact with people who had returned after working at Pullman, or with their relatives.

It is well demonstrated that I got good response to my inquiries. Those who had the kindness to answer were impressed with the Pullman cars; some had made visits there, others had relatives who worked there, and some had pictures from there in photo albums. The carpenters profession was evident. In one case a poster on the wall telling that Pullman wanted carpenters was the reason for making that choice, but in several cases the awareness of the work opportunity had come by mouth. Someone had said there were good possibilities.

The two individual destinies as described, bring attention to the great connection.

The preserved letters give us the living conditions from the home surroundings, the journey overseas, the reception, the work, living quarters, impressions, living conditions, free time, love affairs, dreams, traditions, contacts with those at home, and companionship with those who came from the same region.

The information from within the town of Pullman that was more America-emphasized, makes clear where the roots were on arrival to Chicago; family relationships, the Swedish language's position among the elderly, the important role of coffee, the pastors' central mission among the congregations' children, the religious roots they grew up with, the psalmists' words of trust. But also seen from the youths' point of view, Swedes, Irish, Scots, Polish, Croats, Serbs, Slovaks, and Germans, who played football in the parks near the town of Pullman, and the previous representation so aptly characterized:

"The play is intense and brutal, with ethnic hatred brought over from the old country. The spectators are all men, they wear suits, vests and neckties under heavy overcoats, wear felt fedora hats, and smoke cigars.

---

[1] Bread dipped in a pork soup.
[2] A brand of toothpaste.
[3] Servant girl and farm laborer.

George Mortimer Pullman 1831-1897
Founder of the Pullman Palace Car Company in 1867.
Courtesy of My Community *magazine.*

Left: Ernst Åkerberg's parents, Emma and Carl of Ryfors. Photo owned by Tage Åkerberg.
Right: Ernst Åkerberg at 20 years in 1900. Photo Tage Åkerberg.

Lake Street Bridge, Chicago. Postcard Nov. 1905 from Helena Hellstrom to future mother-in-law, Emma Åkerberg. Handwriting on the face of the card reads: "Here is the train we ride on to Pullman. As you see it is well up in the air. Tell Ida I would be so happy if she would write to me sometime. I wish you all a Merry Christmas and a Happy New year. Helena." Owned by Tage Åkerberg.

Ernst Åkerberg with three of his companions from Ryfors wearing their Sunday clothes visit the photographer, Banks on Kensington Ave., Chicago. Filip Hillstrom, Karl Hurtig. Seated, August Hurtig and Ernst. Owned by Tage Åkerberg.

The Hillstrom brothers who worked at Pullman. Photo taken in Chicago around 1903-1905. Back row left to right: Pontus, Reinhold, David, Johan, Edward. Front row l-r: Fritiof, Filip, Fingal. Photo owned by Mike Hillstrom.

AND SWEDISH IMMIGRATION

Left, the Johnson family outside their home in Roseland. 1912. Gustav, Anna, daughter Ethel

Right, Raymond E. Johnson's grandfather (father's father), Nils Gustaf Johnson. Although born in Sweden he was known for his "Italian look."
Photos owned by R. E. Johnson.

THE PULLMAN SOCIAL EXPERIMENT

Mrs. Anna Johnson 1862-1955. "Mother to Community."
Photo by Warren Johnson.

Chapter III
The Elim Congregation

Activities

The Swedes first belonged to the Elim congregation. It was organized in 1883, and the church considers 1885 as its inaugural year. Its directors were made up of "lay workers and trustees."

The church was located at the corner of 113th Street and Forest Ave.[1] The nearest cemetery was Oakwoods, near Chicago's Grand Crossing neighborhood.

Thanks to its newspaper, "The Luther Banner Advocate," I have had an insight into its organization and activities.

The morning service took place on Sundays at 10:30 and evening service was at 5:30 p.m. They held bible study on Wednesdays at 7:45 p.m.

The Church's societies were shown as follows:

The women's society, Dorcas, with meetings on Thursdays at 2 p.m.

Luther League, with meetings on the 1st and 3rd Thursday evenings at 8 o'clock.

Talita Kumi, young women's society with meetings on the 2nd Thursday, 8:15 p.m.

Confirmation group, with meetings the last Friday of the month at 7:45, from October to May.

The men's choir, with rehearsals on Tuesdays at 7:00 p.m.

Miriam, when banns are published.

The church choir, Tuesdays at 8:15 p.m.

Bethel society, the men's sick visitation society, 1st Friday night of the month.

Bethesda, the women's sick visitation, 1st Friday of the month 8:00 p.m.

Weekday school, every summer during July and August in the church classroom.

This is certainly an impressive list of activities. Some parts of the designations call for a more detailed explanation, but most are quite clear.

Elim was a camp area during Israel's desert wandering with "12 wells and 70 palm trees," Exodus, 15:27 and Numbers, 33:9.

Talita Kum was a word denoting power. Mark 5:14, 7:34. Compare with Ephatha, "open up."

Dorcas was devoted to charity, and had made garments. Peter awakened her from the dead. Acts, 9:36.

Miriam was a sister of Moses and Aaron.

Raymond E. Johnson has just told us of Pastor Tengwald, and Ernst Åkerberg of the visit to the church by the men of Nykyrke. When the congregation's first pastor died in 1911, on the 9th of December, the obituary notice clearly revealed that he had been a central figure, not only for the Swedes in the town of Pullman but also for others among them and for many in other Lutheran congregations in the USA.

Pastor Zetterstrand, mentioned earlier, was born in Värna, Östergötland, on March 6, 1863, and was the son of the organist and scholar, Jonas Petter Johansson and his wife Ulrika Eleonora Zetterstrand. He attended the secondary school in Linköping between 1873-1880. After one year's service as a private tutor and several as a pharmaceutical student, he emigrated from Stockholm to the USA in the spring of 1884. Already in the fall term of the same year he enrolled in Augustana College. Three years later he became a student of the classics and after three years of theological studies he was ordained together with 18 other candidates in 1889 in Moline, Illinois. Most of them worked in the service of the synod. Zetterstrand's first mission was the Salem congregation in Creston, Iowa. In the fall of 1891 he received the call to Elim congregation in Pullman. Later he was also attached to Augustana College as a teacher. His last call was to Salem congregation in Naugatuck, Connecticut, where he died in 1911. He was mourned foremost by his wife, Helena Elizabeth, born Öhman, and seven children, and among his siblings, one brother, Pastor Jonasson in Mjölby. The congregation expressed its thankfulness to him that, through his talents, he was able to accomplish so much within the area of the town of Pullman. His physician was the well-known doctor in New Britain, Connecticut, E. T. Fromén.

At his passing the shops in Naugatuck were closed and the flags on the public buildings were lowered to half staff. In the mourners procession 20 priests took part. The president of the New York conference, W.F. Jacobson spoke on the topic, "A true servant of Christ." Pastor E.C. Bloomquist preached in English on Jesus' words, "Lazarus, our friend sleeps." An American friend of the family then lowered him to his final resting place.

I will now have a closer look at Elim congregation's yearly meetings; first the one held in January, 1912, in which it was reported that the morning services were nearly always well filled. The worship at evening services had, on the other hand, not been so well attended, which gave rise to the conclusion that they should hold every other service in English. It was suggested that Wednesday evening meetings be discontinued and that the pastor should instead, make visits to homes in Pullman town on those evenings.

The Sunday school counted no less than 350 children and 30 teachers, but teaching in North Pullman was suspended, and the children there had to come instead to South Pullman and its church. In 1911, fifty-four young people were confirmed, which was reported to be the largest confirmation class in the congregation's history.

The congregation board had 11 meetings that year; the church council met upon call of the chairman, and the trustees met every month. Anna W. Johnson took care of the duties of organist and Fritiof Hillstrom led the choir which consisted of 32 members. Singing during Julotta [Christmas service] was considered to have been the most inspirational ever heard in this church. The Dorcas society had supported the costs of renovating the parsonage.

The congregation's treasurer, Axel Mureen announced that income at the year's end was $3,958 and expenses were $3,668. The congregation's pastor, G.K. Stark was the board chairman with P.J.D. Lyckberg (10529 Corliss Ave.) as secretary and John Oman (11140 Indiana Ave.) as caretaker. The Elim church building stood, as mentioned earlier, at 113th Street and Forest Ave.

The businesses that supported Elim church by advertising in *The Luther Banner* were: The Pullman Trust and Savings Bank, The Roseland State Bank, 115th St. and Michigan Ave., Lundberg's Furniture, 11215-17 Michigan Ave., Carl A. Sandstrom Real Estate, 11250 Michigan Ave., Lindquist's shoes, 11308 Michigan Ave., Swedish Washington Park Hospital, 60th St. and Vernon Ave., Bethel Burial help Society of Elim church, Gustaf Bloom, Grocer, 148 W. 113th, E. Karlson Shoes, 11121 Michigan Ave., also K. Thureson Shoes, 11134 Michigan Ave., Pearson and Malmström watchmakers and jewelers, 11340 Michigan Ave., and Holden Swanson Dry Goods, 113th St. and Michigan Ave. The town's doctors were: O. Olson, Alfred Hakanson, eye, ear, nose, and throat specialist, and the dentists were: G. T. Alm and Horace Tharp, both had practices on Michigan Avenue, the main street.

Advertisements in The Luther Banner

The Members

It is now necessary to introduce *questions* about the congregation's children, starting with where they lived.

To answer these questions I have gone through *Churchbook of The Swedish Evangelical Lutheran Elim Congregation, Pullman, Illinois, 1887-1893,*, page 1-89 and *Ministerial Acts,* 1886-1919.

The books were microfilmed by Lennart Setterdahl for the Swedish Emigrant Institute.

A review of them shows that the most Swedes lived on Stevenson Ave. Kensington Ave.,took 2nd place, Fulton St., 3rd, Cottage Grove Ave., 4th, Erickson Ave. 5th, Grand Crossing [neighborhood] 6th, and blocks A-F.,7th place.

A review of them also shows the following as big recruiting regions: Göteborg, Borås and Lidköping, Horn in Östergötland, Glimåkra in Kristianstads län, Högby, Hovby, and Öljehult in Blekinge län, Högsäter, Färgelanda, Frändefors and Ödeborg in Dalsland, and Håcksvik in Älvsborgs län, Nykyrke, N. Åsarp and Luttra in Skaraborgs län, Högby and Böda on Öland in Kalmar län and Valbo in Gästrikland.

In the membership list which began before 1886 I found names of families and single members which I will now present:

The Södergren family from *Göteborg*. Its provider Otto Waldemar was born 04/09/1862 and his wife Anna Christina 05/14/1861. The children were five, Wilhelm Otto b. 03/27/1884, Hugo Evald b.07/06/1888, Johan Alfred Waldemar b. 12/10/1894, Oscar Gustaf Herbert b. 06/29/1896, and Nanna Emilia b. 04/14/1900.

The Andrew Peterson family from *Borås*. He was born 09/01/1846, his wife Maria Carolina 02/28. Her maiden name was Bengtsson. They had two children, both born in Pullman, Johan Henning 05/01/1883 and Ebba Christina 10/18/1886.

Arvid Pontus Peterson and Henry Johnson from *Borås*. Their birth dates were 11/18/1878 and 08/06/1879. They lived on Stevenson St., then at the corner of Erickson street and Cottage Grove. Erik Mattias Peterson b. 02/25/1879 is registered there, actually a friend of Arvid Pontus.

The Johnson family from Runsten, Kalmar län. Pehr August was born on 10/24/1863 and Charlotta on 11/16/1863. She was from Karlslunda, also in Kalmar. They had five children who were born in Pullman, Hulda Theresia, b. 09/26/1889, Axel Fridolf b. 01/21/1891, Victor Rudolf, b. 04/29/1894, Florence Victoria, b. 01/17/1897 and Emma Augusta Charlotta, b. 06/06/1900.

The Lars Peter Larson family from Sanda, Gotland. He was born on 10/29/1849 and his wife, Amanda Laurentia Peterson on 07/23/1856. Of the three children, Hilma Sofia and Gerda were born in Klinte in 1873 and 1881, resp. On 08/04/1892 they had a little sister who was baptized Fanny Mia Elisabeth.

The family Gustaf Magnus Hård were from Bergsjö in Hälsingland. Gustaf Magnus was born on 12/23/1860. His wife was named Matilda with the maiden name Anderson. Her date of birth is not known. They had eight children; seven girls, Helena Maria, Emma Louisa, Alma Christina, Ida Victoria, Bertha Matilda, Augusta Margareta, Charlotta, Elizabeth, and finally a son, Carl Gustaf Adolf. The oldest child was born in Sweden, several in Buffalo, N.Y., and both of the youngest in Chicago. The family emigrated from Bergsjö to Buffalo, where Gustaf Magnus found work at Pullman, apparently a rather good thing when they had to provide for such a large family. They lived on 113th Street in Pullman.

Among the more uncommon names (found in the index) we find such as Bolm from Ödeborg in Dalsland; Leman from Stockholm; Johan Anton Gustaf born 08/28/1884; Lagerholm, Ivar also from Stockholm; Borén, Sten Otto b.06/14/1879 in Horns parish Östergötland; Fritiof Hellström from Nykyrke in Skaraborgs län b.12/31/1874, as we already know from the section on the Åkerbergs from this parish. Benander, Carl Albin b. 03/26/1878 in Högsäter in Dalsland; Swanton, Johan, widower, born 1825 in Svenarums parish in Jönköpings län; Norström, Carl Peter Hugo b.10/08/1864 in Westkinde on Gotland; Timgren, also from Gotland. Peter August b.12/02/1865 in Roma parish; Känström, Anna Katarina, widow, b.07/16/1828 and Paulus b.01/25/1868 in Håksviks parish in Sjuhäradsbygden; Sandström, Carl August and Sven Erland from Högsby in Kalmar län, born 08/09/1857 and 03/28/1868 resp. Ahlberg, two brothers, August and Magnus from Öljehult in Blekinge, born 09/24/1862 and 01/02/1865; Swensén, Carl from Munkarp in Skåne, b.05/02/1865; Germundson, Johannes from Stenbrohult, b. 10/23/1865; Selldén, Peter Johan Johanson from Torsås, Kronobergs län, b.04/18/1869; also a Hellström from Mullsjö. This time Gustaf Fingal, b.11/16/1870; Person, Anders Vilhelm from Horn b.01/31/1872; Broling. Anders Johan from "Elfsborg" b.02/17/1873; Rapp, Carl J. from "Kronoberg", b.01/02/1872; Nyman, Gustaf Harry from Lidköping, b.06/03/1870; Morén, Anders Gabriel Kristofferson from Moheda, b.12/14/1864; Rapp, Anders Gustaf from Berga, also Kronobergs län, b.12/13/1866; Lindell, Karl Johan from Ervalla in Örebro län, b.12/01/1856; Tedén, Carl Johan from Skölvene in Sjuhäradsbygden, b.11/08/1846; Berggren, Hans Petter, from Höganäs, b.09/20/1860; Sandström, Samuelsson Frans Alfred from Vist in Östergötland, b.03/04/1863; Molin, Gustaf Adolf from Börstig in Skaraborgs län, b. 07/16/1874; Myrén, Nils Nilsson from Brunskog in Värmland, b.03/08/1868; Lenander, Gustaf Julius Artur from Örtomta in Östergötland, b.07/11/1873; Strand, Johan Magnus from Almundsryd in Kronobergs län, b. 09/21/1878; Fridell, Johan Larsson from Mellby in Skaraborgs län, b.12/22/1866; Ågren, Kurt Robert from Hoby in Blekinge, b. 12/31/1870; Lundell, Carl A. from Arvika, b.07/05/1863; Engström, Frank from Värmskog, b.09/12/1868; Sjöblom, Beda and Ada from Vårgårda, born 12/13/1863 and 12/02/1866; The widow Lönnquist, Sigrid Christina from Nässjö, b.05/02/1828; and the widow Hedberg, Maria Christina, b. 11/07/1837.

What do we know then of the church's services, baptisms, confirmations, weddings, etc.?

Out of preserved statistics for the years 1886-1892 these observations can be made.

The numbers of baptisms were: 33 in 1886, 57 in 1887, 46 in 1888, 68 in 1889, 72 in 1890, 38 in 1891 and 95 in 1892.

The numbers of confirmed were: 0 in 1886, 3 in 1887, 9 in 1888, 11 in 1889, 10 in 1890, 7 in 1891, 11 in 1892.

Recorded marriages were: 8 in 1886, 7 in 1887, 10 in 1888, 12 in 1889, 13 in 1890, 7 in 1891, 24 in 1892.

The numbers of newly-enrolled members were: 57 in 1886, 23 in 1887, 43 in 1888, 7 in 1889, 8 in 1890, 69 in 1891, 75 in 1892, The numbers moved away were: 8 in 1886, 10 in 1887, 9 in 1888, 8 in 1889, 3 in 1890, 4 in 1891, 12 in 1892.

The numbers who withdrew from the congregation were: 8 in 1886, 10 in 1887, 9 in 1888, 8 in 1889, 3 in 1890, 0 in 1891, 22 in 1892. The numbers who died were; 4 in 1886, 5 in 1887, 4 in 1888, 3 in 1889, 2 in 1890, 2 in 1892, 6 in 1892.

The partakers of holy communion were: 35 (3/6) 1887, 21 (6/7) 1887, 20 (9/8) 1887, 22 (12/4) 1887, 16 (3/10) 1888, 16 (4/11) 1888, 20 (6/10) 1888, 26 (9/13) 1888, 53 (12/23) 1888, 13 (3/15) 1889, 27 (6/16) 1889, 10 (7/17) 1889, 20 (9/18) 1889, 25 (12/19) 1889, 35 (3/20) 1890, 25 (4/6) 1890, 22 (6/22) 1890, 21 (9/23) 1890, 30 (11/24) 1890, 45 (3/25) 1891, 40 (6/7) 1891, 52 (10/27) 1891, 25 (11/28) 1891, 57 (3/29) 1892, 42 (5/30) 1992, 46 (8/31) 1892, 35 (10/22) 1892, 41 (12/23) 1892.

The statistics above are from accounts in *Ministerial Acts* by Rev. Zetterstrand.

The names

An examination of Christian names and second names that parents gave their children from 1885 to 1892 in the Elim congregation, show the following:

Anna, Amalia, Amanda, Augusta, Beda, Carolina, Charlotta, Christina, Clara, Ebba, Elin, Elisabeth, Emma, Ester, Hilda, Hildur, Ida, Jenny, Maria, Mathilda, Olga, Selma seem to have been common.

Likewise with Alfred, Axel, Carl, Edwin, Ernst, Gustaf, Johan, Leo, Nils, Oscar, Sven, Walter and Victor.

Most popular were Anna, Augusta, Beda, Clara, Elin, Ester, Ida, Jenny. Carl, Edwin, Gustaf, Johan, Nils, Oscar, Sven.

Names more common to the new world preference were such as the following. As a rule it is believed that they were the results of "intermarriages."

1886

Rosie, Henry, Charlie, Frank, George, Hazel, Elsie, Ralph.

1887

Mabel, Eveline, Georgina, Clifford

1889

Florence, Roy, Rosie, Emroy, Virginia

1890

Sadie, Effie, Richard, Ruth, Girthie, Melie

1891

Mary, Clarence, Carrie, Methel

1892

Mervin, Rhody, Grover, Stanley, Norman

Names of a strange character also occur, such as the following. I show them as the closest examples in the sequence in which they appear in the baptism lists.

1886

Mercidese, Olga Mercides, Leontine

1888

Assaria, Lilly Assaria, Serafia, Ruth Serifia

1889

Torbania, Martha Rosine Torbania, Almira, Ruth Almira

1892

Hartinius, Hartinius Ferdinand Linneus, Arthur Linneus

In Sweden a statistical table of names was drawn up by Karin and Sven Norrman and published in *Swedish Dialects*, 1988. According to them the most common baptismal names were these:

Maria, Charlotta, Anna, Sofia, Augusta, Elisabet, Karolina, Lovisa, Fredrika, Katarina, Carl, Gustaf, Johan, Fredrik, Vilhelm, Axel, August, Otto, Adolf, Erik, Anders, Nils, Olof, Per.

At the end of the 19th Century the taste in Sweden turned towards shorter names, some of which could not have been familiar to the Elim congregation. Some of the best known were Greta, Signe, Karin, Ester, Gunnar, Bror, Knut, Nils, Sven.

Among more modern names during the 20th Century in Sweden, Roland Otterbjörk in *Swedish First Names*, 1964, p. 55, lists these: Britta, Eva, Inga, Mona, Pia, Ulla Åsa, Arne, Börje, Göte, Ove, Rune, Tage, Tore.

Karin and Sven Norrman ascribed the time of double names to 1890-1930, such names as Anna-Greta, Ann-Britt, Maj-Lis, Karl-Erik, Karl-Gustav, Karl-Olof. Examples of double names are found, consequently, throughout the American material.

As before, a common background can also be mentioned that the most common first names, Christian names, and second names now used in Sweden, according to Sture Allén and Staffan Wåhlin in *The First Name Book*, 1995, are the following:

Maria, Anna, Margareta, Eva, Elisabet, Karin, Kristina, Birgitta, Elisabeth, Ingrid, Marie, Kerstin, Linnea, Marianne, Christina. Erik, Karl, Lars, Anders, Per, Johan, Lennart, Nils, Gunnar, Sven, Olof, Jan, Hans, Bengt, Mikael.

And the most common Christian names given children born as late as 1995 are these:

Emma, Elin, Amanda, Hanna, Sara, Linnea, Julia, Johanna, Rebecka, Josefine, Emelie, Mathilda, Sofia, Frida, Anna.

Markus, Oscar, Erik, Simon, Viktor, Alexander, Filip, Anton, Emil, Johan, Jonatan, Daniel, Andreas, Jesper, Sebastian.

In summing up it is clear that Anna and Maria, Carl and Gustaf were just as popular in the Elim congregation as in the old country.

Ida and Jenny, Edvin and Oskar demonstrate that most parents in the new country held great love for those in the old.

Maria and Anna seem to have remained through the years as have Karl and Johan.

It will also be observed that Emma and Amanda have made a comeback.

But in this connection it is, of course, most interesting to see the American names that parents in Elim congregation gave their children:

Fanny, Florence, Girthie, Jenny, Rosie, Clarence, Grover, Norman, Roy, Stanley, among others.

We consider that the last name can establish that the common name types from that time are representative, with the exception of names of the nobility. There are, for example, the "son"- names, which began to be permanent (hereditary) with the rural people during the later part of the 1880 decade. There are also many typical middle class family names such as, Södergren, Leman, Lagerholm,

Hellström, Norrström, Tungren, Känström, Ahlberg, Nyman, Berggren, Sandström, Ågren. Such use contains a natural characteristic inspired by a place name. Also, one could merely have chosen a name that pleased him. We had no rules about family names before 1901, when the first lists came. Even the few single middle class names such as Strand are represented. The so-called academic names are also encountered, for example, Benander, Swensén, Selldén, Morén, Lindell, Tedén, Molin, Lenander, Fridell. Perhaps Rapp and Hård are examples of soldier names.

Interesting is the example of women having a permanent son-name. According to the old way she would use dotter [daughter] instead. The question of when and why an Alma Andersdotter became fru [Mrs.] Alma Johansson has not so far been thoroughly investigated. This happened obviously during the later part of the 19th Century. It is also interesting to notice the use taken by women of the man's family name. Women born with their own family name normally, in old times, retained it after marriage. Transition to a common family name for a legitimate wife is in part a rather young phenomenon. Use of a common family name first developed during the 1880 decade. The first official instructions in Sweden for the name community of wives was in a 1915 ordinance.

In my analysis of names I have had contact with the head of research, Eva Brylla at the place-name archive in Uppsala.

In an interview in *Svenska Dagbladet* of 01/16/1998, made by Anna-Lena Wik-Thorsell, Eva Brylla could also give examples of first names in school catalogs. It further mentions that parents' choice of names for their children reflects their life styles and their expectations for their children and often also their interests. She further cited Ronny Ambjörnsson in his autobiographical essay, *My First Name is Ronny,* that his name reveals his class origins: "In elementary school there were several Ronnys, in secondary grammar school I was alone. And in high school there was a Kent and a Gilbert, both as odd as I in a milieu dominated by Anders, Per, and Krister."

Trends

At the close of this chapter let me now identify and place the Elim congregation in a comparative grouping. In 1982 Karl A. Olsson discussed the continuity and conversion within the Swedish immigrants' societies in the USA, and confirmed the founding dates of some of the organizations: Scandinavian Methodism 1846; Swedish Lutherans 1849; Augustana Synod 1860, The Lutheran Church in America; Swedish Baptists 1852, The Baptist General Conference 1879; The Scandinavian Free Churches 1884, The Evangelical Free Church 1950, The Swedish Mission Alliance in America 1868, Evangelical Covenant Church 1873. The Elim Congregation in Pullman belonged to the Augustana Synod, which was actually Sweden's largest religious community outside the homeland.

I assumed that in Gunnar Westin's work, *The Emigrants and the Church, Letters to and from Swedes in America 1849-1892,* I would find descriptions of life in the congregations from which I could expand my picture of Elim Congregation, but his selections illustrate mostly the "Swedish-American" churches' influx from the motherland, "particularly the clerical recruiting", page 6. Nor is there in his magnum opus, *The History of Protestantism in the United States of America,* 1931, anything about it to be found. J. V. Berger emphasizes, in his *Our Church, The Swedish-American Ecclesiastical Relationships, Seen From the National and Populist Point of View,* 1912, just what I noted in Pastor Zetterstrand and his colleagues in Pullman, namely, how the congregation's history had certainly been that of their priests.

It was the priests who led in the funding of church buildings, organized the congregation's different committees, led the bazaars and provided for the appearance of guest speakers.

As an example of name information I came across in material other than that cited, I will also reproduce several examples from a book named, *The Greater Roseland Area of Chicago,* edited by Janice Helge and published by the South Suburban Genealogical and Historical Society. It consists of a compilation of "Society News" out of local newspapers from Pullman-Roseland-Kensington-Calumet-Gano in the year 1909. The contents are brief accounts of travels and invitations etc. Among others, these are extracted from pages 1-34: (In original sequence: they are alphabetized in the index).

Mrs. Gothard Dahlberg 112th and State St.; O. R. Hillstrom; E. O. Carlson; Miss Jennie Lundberg, 11315 Prairie Ave.; Mrs Harriet Olson and Florence Nylander; Mrs James Aurelius, Mrs Hildebrand; Mr Ruben Aderberg, 159 W. 109th St.; Mr Lindquist; Mrs Mary Beckman; Mr Benjamin Lundberg, 11222 Michigan Ave. Mr Nils G. Carlson, 725 W. 120th St.

Here also is to be found lists of brothers of the order in the Pullman-Roseland Fides Lodge 842, chartered October 1895. The Historic Pullman Foundation archives has collected this information. Among Swedes who are listed in the years 1913-1926, page 64-68 are the following:

Fredrik Walter Anderson, Oscar L. Carlson, Albert E. Carlson, N. G. Erickson, Abel A. E. Erickson, Frank T. L. Erickson, Eric B. Gustafson, Harold C. L. Larson, Charles A. Larson, Elmer Th. Larson, John G. Lofgren, David A. Lund, Ivar Carl Olson, Julius R. Paulsen, Gottfried Ferdinand Peterson, Hans Peter Selander, August Gideon Thompson.

Most of the priests mentioned had been influenced by Fjellstedt, Rosenius and Ahlberg, which means that their general bent was pietistic. Lars Ljungmark believes to that effect in *The Great Emigration*, 1965, page 159, that in the beginning the congregations were largely reminded of the homeland. As soon as they got their own priest, they often built a church. The need of fellowship had meant much for the establishment of different religious communities. Even if that need of the following generations was not as strong, yet the religious pattern of behavior was preserved. After a certain time Swedish-Americans would now and then leave their churches and enter some American congregation, like "The Episcopal Church" and thus be rid of the "disdained stamp of the immigrant."

The congregations in Chicago often aligned themselves with the temperance movement. Already in 1868 a Swedish KFUM was founded by leaders from the Augustana churches. The congregations also offered Christian alternatives to the sickness and burial welfare societies. Even if the seekers of fellowship and safety had nothing to do with education or class consciousness, it was considered, according to observations made in Chicago by Ulf Beijbom in *Emigrants and Swedish-America*, 1966, that the founding of congregations had been the specialty of business men or craftsmen who had attained advancement in the society of immigrants, page 141.

In 1910 Elim congregation celebrated its 25 year jubilee. It still can be read in *Bekännaren* Jan., 1911, page 1ff, under the headline, "Our jubilee celebration Dec 2-4, 1910."

> The unanimous testimony of the festival was that there was much success with the great music, speeches, and preaching. In the center stood the congregations' pastor, G. K. Stark, together with his predecessors in office, Pastor, E. A. Zetterstrand, G. A. Ekeberg, H. G. Lindblad, and V. J. Tengwald. The one missing was Pastor G. Forsberg, who had died. Zetterstrand and Tengwald we know from earlier mentions. One might call it a touching contribution when G. A. Ekeberg read the list of names which he had written in the first secretary book: "Those who were there stood up when their names were read and more than one eye was in tears."

> From a timid start it was considered that the congregation worked itself up to "esteem and prosperity," with Sunday school, confirmation instruction, and many activities groups. The congregations' own organist led the musical selections. Elim's "Echo Quartet" played. Carl A. Lindgren sang a solo number, and the festival speech was given by E. A. Zetterstrand on the subject, "Disappointments and harvests gathered during a 25 year sowing."

> When the church was also renovated for the jubilee, the signatory L.L. ended his article about the fest day in this way: "Those who have not seen the newly beautified church at Pullman do not know how inviting and homelike the church is now, perhaps the most pleasant of any churches we have in Chicago."

At the beginning of the century the congregation consisted of between 600-800 members, of whom most were connected to the Pullman car shops and lived in Pullman or in the neighboring Roseland. I think, after a number of those had stood when their names were read, they almost had a vision before them—of whole rows of pews with Pullman workers and their families, who stood there in their Sunday clothes in the newly renovated, flower—bedecked church; particularly of all the skilled carpenters with wives and children and parents, relatives and friends: Åkerbergs, Hellströms, Johnsons, Bensons, Bergströms, Carlsons, Nordlunds, Nordstrands, Norlins, Pearsons, Ströms, Sundells and many others whose names have been mentioned earlier.

Additional names of carpenters from our region are found, moreover, in a list of those belonging to the Vasa Order of America, lodge 128, Chicago, in Swedens Emigrant Archive, Växjö, Sweden:

John E. Anderson from Öland
Erick Berg from Ytterhogdal
Oscar Bork from Bohuslän
Axel F. N. Carlson from Småland
Linus Carlson from Bohuslän
Ludvig Carlson from Grängesberg
Oscar Carlson from Nässjö
Bernhard Domey from Årnäs
Carl Oscar Erikson from Ramsberg
Adrian Gustafson from N. Möckleby
Carl Gustafson from Svenarum
Ernst Helge from Skärblacka
Albin Johnson from Möckleby
Carl Johnson from Runsten

Johan D. Johnson from Ängelholm
Verner Johnson from Ransäter
Anton W. Lindell from Huaröd
Carl Emil Olson from Halmstad
Tage Olson from Torslunda
Ludvig Pearson from Knäred
Ivar Schöning from Ovanåker
Arvid Sjöholm from Hudiksvall
Carl Swanson from Torpa
M. Swanson from Rödeby
Olle Swanson from Småland
Emil Swenson from Kristianstad
Manfred Sundström from Öland

To go further in the congregation's history, on April 25-30, 1916, the Illinois Conference for the Swedish Evangelical Lutheran Churches was held at Elim Church in Pullman. According to the Luther Banner for May-June the congregation accommodated "the large crowd in a grand manner."

In the same year, however, certain warning signals were heard. In the annual report it was written accordingly: "Because of the large movement away from this district our congregation is suffering more than a little. If working conditions do not become better at the Pullman shops, it may be that the number of Swedes may be significantly reduced. All congregation members in this area are suffering because of the shops' changeable labor position. Businessmen in this area complain vigorously to the Pullman Company that the condition, due to their blood sucking system, has driven away the better class of working people to be replaced by workers from Southern Europe."

To my knowledge, this is the first time that criticism has been directed in any annual report from the congregation toward the Pullman Shop's policies on working conditions, and the first time we see a reaction against the renting of Pullman town dwellings to South Europeans.

The trend appeared clearly in the following annual report. Stated accordingly in 1917, for example, is the church's position in the town's plans: "Another thing that I (the Pastor) wish is that our congregation shall take into consideration that, although our church has the nicest location one could wish for, yet it is no longer a central position. Most of the Swedish people now live west of Michigan Ave., and northward as far as 100th Street. This makes it extremely difficult to bring people to our services.

On that year, or 1918, a new pastor took over, Carl A. Tolin, and he reported on New Years Day, 1919, that a serious influenza epidemic was ravaging during the autumn of 1918, and that only 14 children were enrolled in the reading class compared to 38 in the last, but "The agony of death which during the days of the great war burdened the heart and senses, has likewise served to give hopeful joy with a brighter look to the future." He also took up the question of language and wrote that on July 7, for the first time, communion was held exclusively in the English language.

January 16, 1931 is the last dated report in the material Lennart Setterdahl microfilmed. The depression had then put its stamp on jobs, workers, and the congregation. Thus, not only was a person held in the grip of the times, but the crippled congregation was also marked with dissension. Consequently, the pastor at the beginning of the 30s-decade, G. Ahnquist, concluded his remarks in this way:

> Destructive criticism and words that reveal a small and narrow view are altogether out of place. They hurt whenever spoken and not least do they hurt when directed to a pastor and his wife. By such words they easily become discouraged and unfitted for the challenging task they are called upon to do.

Neither could the town of Pullman rise up again during the three long decades before "The Historic Pullman Foundation" was established, by those who realized the value of preserving Pullman town. We are now standing at the year 1973. Elim Lutheran Church had then changed its name to "Reformation Lutheran Church," and the congregation was now comprised of "black people" for the most part.[2]

The same changes came to other Swedish churches in Roseland. The Swedish Baptist Church of Roseland was founded in 1882 and stood at 111th and Edbrooke Ave.

The Swedish Evangelical Mission Church, later the Free Church, was located at 11032 Indiana Ave. The congregation celebrated its 75-year Jubilee in 1957. The Superintendent 1895-1908 was A. J. Norrman. His sermons were distinguished by his gestures and warmth. The founders were, among others, Carl Nordell, Swan Peterson, G. Brodin, Charles Blomberg, H. Enger, and John Lundin.

Pullman, the shops and town seen from Roseland in 1886.
At the left, power house, water tower, chimney, clock tower.

From 1882 to 1890 the congregation rented a room in the Pullman Arcade. In 1891 they built their church on Indiana Ave. From Jan Helge and Paula Malak, *Churches of the Greater Roseland (Chicago) Area* (South Holland, IL: South Suburban Genealogical & Historical Society, 1988).

Roseland Swedish Methodist was founded in 1917 and stood at 113th and Indiana. When these congregations were organized they were located in the Pullman Arcade Building. The majority of Swedes belonged to the Elim congregation, whose archives are also the best preserved. From the Methodists I received the message, "No early records and no early history."

This chapter has consequently been illuminated by what was conscripted from the children of the congregation–where they lived, what they were named, how baptisms, confirmations and weddings can be read from the material and what names the parents gave their children at baptism, the trends, and much more.

My endeavor throughout has been to reconcile the general and the specific: Activities, Membership, Characteristics.

G. M. Pullman was undeniably one of those "Captains of Industry" who demanded obedience and discipline. His great project was created as a welfare community.

Swedes were known for their reliability. It was characteristic of them to educate themselves, to be conscious of Swedish-American culture–compare Dag Blanck in *Becoming Swedish-American*, 1997.

Between Pullman and Henry Ford (1863-1947) one can perhaps also draw a parallel. His factories were also built after a model, and within the automobile industry the appeal was to the capacity of man to consider himself in the land of the future just as Gösta Arvastson shows in *Rig* 1998, no. 4 page 204. In Dearborn, Michigan, Ford had a map they used for home visits. Interest in jazz, short skirts, and smoking were not to be permitted.

To the right, Hotel Forence, Arcade, and Greenstone church.
From Our Community, *Vol. no. 3, 1958. A publication of the Pullman Trust and Savings Band, Chicago.*

[1] The Elim Swedish Lutheran Church originally met in rented space in the Arcade Building according to my grandmother, Anna Hedberg Johnson, a charter member. The church itself was the first, other than the Greenstone, to be built with the support of George M. Pullman. The land at 113th and Calumet Avenue in Roseland was donated. At about the same time Pullman donated land across 113th Street for the Holy Rosary Catholic Church. Solon Beman was the architect for both.
In 1905, Elim church had to be moved to its present location at the southwest corner of 113th and Forest Ave. to make way for the construction of Palmer Park.

[2] Elim Lutheran and Peoples Lutheran Church at 110th and State Street, also in Roseland, were merged to form Reformation Lutheran Church. The records of both churches are at Reformation, still located at 113th and Forest Ave.

Elim Lutheran Church, 1996, now Reformation Lutheran. Photo R. E. Johnson.

1 *2907*	2	3	4	5	6
7	8	9	10	11	12

CHICAGO, July 1.6 .....19.17.

THE PULLMAN COMPANY,

HAVING BEEN ADVISED OF THE POLICY OF THE COMPANY WITH RELATION TO INVENTIONS MADE BY ITS EMPLOYES, I AGREE, IN CONSIDERATION OF THE SALARY OR WAGES PAID TO ME, THAT ANY INVENTION OR IMPROVEMENT MADE BY ME DURING THE PERIOD OF MY EMPLOYMENT RELATING IN ANY WISE TO THE BUSINESS OF THE PULLMAN COMPANY, ITS MACHINERY, EQUIPMENT, PROCESSES, METHODS OR PRODUCTS, SHALL BE ASSIGNED TO THE COMPANY, AND TO PROMPTLY DISCLOSE EVERY SUCH INVENTION OR IMPROVEMENT TO THE COMPANY, AND TO EXECUTE ALL PROPER DOCUMENTS NECESSARY IN THE MAKING OF APPLICATIONS FOR PATENTS THEREFOR, TOGETHER WITH AN ASSIGNMENT THEREOF TO THE COMPANY, AND TO GIVE ALL TESTIMONY, AID AND ASSISTANCE NECESSARY TO THE ESTABLISHING OF THE TITLE OF SAID COMPANY IN CASE OF ANY INTERFERENCE, INFRINGEMENT OR OTHER CONTEST RELATIVE TO SUCH INVENTION, WHETHER ARISING DURING MY EMPLOYMENT OR SUBSEQUENT THERETO.

Charles Kjellander
SIGN NAME IN FULL

CHECK NO. *2901*

WITNESS / DEPT. / Labor / DEPT.

CHECK NO. *2901*

WITNESS / DEPT. / Labor / DEPT.

Form M116 2M (WP)Co

A Page out of Carl Kjellander's employment contract, 07/16/1918. Owned by Margit Kjellander Storm, Uniformsgatan 6, Västerås. Carl was her grandfather. He was born in 1857 in Skettilljunga and died in Chicago, 10737 Wabash Ave. At Pullman he was a labor foreman in the steel department.

The Swedish Evangelical Mission Church, 11032 Indiana Ave. Later the Free Church. Photo by Janice Helge.

Chapter IV
Natives of Ryfors at Home and Abroad

Abroad

It must have been a great day for the Hellströms, Åkerbergs, Hurtigs, Spångs, and all the others in the "Ryfors Club of Chicago" when on Sunday the 27th of May, 1922 all those from Ryfors in Pullman and Chicago, received an invitation from Leo and Vera Sager of Ryfors, son and daughter-in-law of the mill manager, Robert Sager.

Leo Sager then served as the legation secretary in Washington. He was born in 1889 and his wife, Vera Brunner, in 1895. Leo was the son of Robert Sager, born in 1850. They spent their childhood years in Ryfors. In 1827 Robert's father acquired the mill in Skaraborgs land near the border of Jönköpings land. Robert became the legation secretary in Paris, first secretary in the ministry of foreign affairs, chief of protocol, and much more. During his diplomatic term in Paris he studied with the architect J.P.R. Letoux. He also owned the Sager house on Strömgatan in Stockholm, which he and Letoux designed in 1893. He married Marie Moltke-Huitfeldt, born 1853. The brother Edvard once served as Head Master of the Stables and married Ida Fock in 1891. After his brother's death in 1919 Edward took over control and management in Ryfors.

One of the Hellströms, G. Fingal, wrote a poem about Leo and Vera Sager's visit to Chicago. Even today it portrays for us the atmosphere within the Ryfors colony on that occasion. The poem is titled, "Memories of Youth in Ryfors," and it was dedicated in honor of the day to Lieutenant and Mrs. Leo Sager. It was sung to the melody "Du Gamla, Du Fria...."[1]

The poem contained 19 verses and recalled to memory glimpses of the mutual community; Ryfors, the mill, the park, the work, the holidays, the Sager family, the factory people, and the rest of the employees.

The poem continued with memories of: Ryfors with its hills and valleys, Lake Stråken, Tidan River, with its sawmills and forges; the seasons, first spring when the cherry trees blossom and the wood anemones are resplendent, and when the pastures and meadows are worked; the summers with haymaking fests on the country estates, and dancing around the maypole and in the barns.

But now they are gathered here, as it states in the 17th verse, under the "star-spangled flag" to honor "Mr. Sager with princely well-wishes to the pair," and for a unanimous "greeting to the Fatherland to send from the many friends of the Sager pair."

A report of the banquet on May 27, 1922 is preserved by the Hellström family which reads as follows: (quoted from the *Luther Banner*)

> A successful banquet was held at the Pullman Club on the 27th of May, when some fifty Westgötlanders gathered to honor mill and land owner Leo Sager and his wife. Mr. Sager, who serves as secretary to the

Swedish Legation in Washington, arrived in company with his young wife here in this country in the beginning of last February and the pair's trip to the United States is also their honeymoon.

Everyone in Chicago from the Westgothia iron works at Ryfors, as one man, attended the said festivities to honor the notable pair, who beforehand expressed a wish, during their visit here, to meet as many of the American residents from Ryfors as possible.

David A. Hillstrom from Corry PA served as master of ceremonies for the evening. Short speeches were made by several of those present, and songs were presented by a male sextet which consisted solely of Westgötlanders. A club had been organized under the name Ryfors Club, whose members meet at least once a year to relive the old memories.

August Hurtig was chosen as chairman, Gustaf Severin as secretary. Lieutenant and Mrs Sager were given honorary membership. Also present were the Superintendent at Pullman Company, A. G. Erickson with his wife, and Nels O. Larsson, who during his visit to Sweden in the year 1900 made the acquaintance of the Lieutenant. At the festival, a telegram of greeting was sent to Lieutenant Sager's mother living in Ryfors, the Countess Maria Sager, born Moltke, and her subsequent answer was received.

Poems and newspaper articles bear witness to the good relations between the leading family, Sager of Ryfors and their employees. They were hailed as "the notable couple," now honorary members of the newly formed club.

No less than 200 persons had emigrated from the Nykyrke parish and 56 came from Ryfors. In Supplement 2 in the back of this book is the list of such persons with the farm they emigrated from, the year, the name, and the stated trade. The lists were compiled in 1975 by Bengt Berglund. The emigration was greatest during the 1880-1890 decade. From the Hellströms' large band of children no less than eleven traveled westward. Only one returned. Several blacksmiths followed the path of emigration. The names Åkerberg and Hurtig we already know from previous pages.

The following year, the Ryfors residents in Chicago made an excursion to Washington Park. It was on the 15th of July, 1923. Songs and poems were also written by G. Fingal Hellström and they contained no less than 37 verses.

They are about the "Sager manor house people" and the Hurtig family, the employee Per Kindlund, Fredrik who drove the milk from Näs, the inspectors Eiserman, Ringman and Zelander, the bookkeepers Uno Carlsson and Engberg, the foreman Åkerberg, Mrs. Elfman, Fina and Clara at the dairy next to the stream, August Samuelsson in the cow house, Jonsson in the yard, the park attendant Holm, the blacksmiths Tiderman and Hurtig, and the journeymen August and Robert, the miller Hellström in Söarp, the tailor Severin, the carpenter Otto, and Lamberg with his son John, and the roof shingle maker Emil Räf and the forester Dahl. One of the final verses reads as follows:

> I could name many more
> from the home up in the north,
> yet just one, your permission I pray,
> on this page to write down,
> for Peter Schultz on native earth
> for industriousness was bred.

From what is described here of the festivities in the town of Pullman and in Chicago in 1922 and 1923 it seems that there was an exceptional feeling of unity among the natives of Ryfors, and there was a cordial atmosphere at the festivities between the natives of Ryfors in the new world and the mill owner gentlefolk from Ryfors.

As the newspaper account said, the "notable pair" expressed its wish to meet as many of the Ryfors-born Americans as possible, and they in their turn truly stood up, embraced the Sagers, and elected them to honorary membership in their club. Moreover, telegrams of greeting were sent during the festivities to the "Lieutenant Sagers by their resident mother in Ryfors."

At Home

Pictures belonging to Nils Hellström and Åke Axell at Mullsjö also show an affinity for excursions on Lake Stråken, hay-making parties for the employees, and the many festivities, some with the village orchestra, at which the Sager family often took part with the mill people and rest of the employees at Ryfors.

Then to the *question* of why so many left this region.

The person having the most knowledge of this is Bengt Berglund, who in his book, *Ryfors Mill 1742-1920*, 1988, gives a complete picture of the situation, P. 158ff.

When the brothers Robert and Edvard Sager came of age in the 1870 decade, it had significance for the Ryfors mill, in that they changed it to a country estate with park-like grounds after the English pattern. The afore-mentioned mill management had other significance during the 30 years that passed after the death of their father, G. M. Sager. Competition from the big steel works had begun to make itself felt and the lesser factories had difficulties finding markets for their iron, but for factories with acreage of arable land and forests the production of iron was supplanted by the increased demand for dressed timber, paper pulp and animal products. Furthermore, the Sager brothers had bought property, built sawmills, dairies, and changed the work opportunities within the agricultural community. The reorganization, however, began to affect many categories of work, the blacksmiths especially. The emigrants were, above all, people from families of up to ten children where the outlook for future support from the factories was not particularly bright.

Furthermore, there was conflict with the present owners' managers which resulted in the emigration of part of the families to Chicago. Johan Wilhelm Hellström (1881) and Oskar Reinhold Hellström (1882) found work rather soon at Pullman. They thrived, wrote home, and, as we have seen from the index, the names of immigrants from Nykyrke, include many from the families Hellström, Åkerberg, and Hurtig, who followed in the first Hellströms' tracks.

If we total up the Nykyrke-born after the emigration years in an organized table, it would look like this. From Supplement 2 at the back of this book.

1852 Carl Fredrik Forsberg, Berget
1852 Gustaf Johansson Lundin, Bosebygd
1852 The Adam Larsson family, Bäckebostugan, Bredared
1863 Axel Andersson, Höryd
1864 The Johan Kjellander family, Bråared
1869 The Sven Andersson family, Halvstenshult, Mullsjö
1869 Carl Levin, Brunskog, Bosebygd
1869 Gustaf Svensson, Sjöryd
1869 Frans Wilhelm J. Sjöberg, Sjöryd
1869 The Johannes Gustafsson family, Björkelund, Halvstenshult
1870 The Alexander Engström family, Maholms garveri
1881 Johan Wilhelm Hellström, Sörarps Kvarn, Ryfors
1881 Johan Gottfrid Andersson, Hultet
1882 Karl Edvard Hellström, Söraps Kvarn, Ryfors
1882 Oskar Reinhold Hellström, Sörarps Kvarn, Ryfors
1886 Gustaf Theodor Bolin, Hultet, Mullsjö
1887 Karl Alfred Ragnar, Ryfors
1887 Per Anders Schultz, Ryfors
1888 Carl Bros, Broberg
1888 Gustaf Fingal Hellström, Sörarps Kvarn, Ryfors

1888 Anna Emilia Hellström, Sörarps Kvarn, Ryfors
1888 Hedda Zackrisson Höryd
1889 Hulda A. Hellström, Sörarps Kvarn, Ryfors
1889 Karl Robert and Gustaf Wilhelm Severin, Ryfors
1889 Ivar Victor Zelander, Ryfors Bruk
1891 Ester Kristina Bolin, Stenhult, Bosebygd
1891 August Fritiof Hellström, Sörarps Kvarn, Ryfors
1892 Johan Alfred, Karl Viktor Aronsson, Aronsdal
1893 The Edvard Landerholm family, Ryfors
1895 Josef Thorulf (Tore) Sandén, Hofmantorp
1898 Karl Albin Forsell, Stranden, Mullsjö
1898 Anna Josefine Svenningsdotter, Skogslund
1898 Gustaf Robert Åkerberg, Ryfors
1899 The Gustaf Schultz family, Ryfors
1900 Frans Augustsson, Ryds kvarn, Ryfors
1900 David Alfrid Hellström, Sörarps Kvarn, Ryfors
1900 Karl Axel Gottfrid Johansson, Utterhaga, Mullsjö
1900 Helfrid Anna Elisabeth Södergren, Ryfors Bruk
1901 August Henrik Hurtig, Ryfors Bruk
1901 Karl Axel Hurtig, Sörarp, Ryfors
1901 Gertrud Sofia Södergren, Ryfors
1902 Ernst Hjalmar Åkerberg, Ersered, Ryfors
1903 Nelly Josefsson, Ryds kvarn, Ryfors
Helena Maria Hellström, Sörarps Kvarn, Ryfors
Anders Filip Hellström, Sörarps Kvarn, Ryfors
1906 Karl Reinhold Hurtig, Ryfors Bruk
1906 Johan Arvid Utterberg, Utterhagen, Mullsjö

As to my *second question* about the carpenters' knowledge, I got the answer that the tenant holdings in Ryfors always required upkeep, and the tenants were naturally among the factory people who were skilled in carpentry.

From the records the regional researcher Åke Axell, Mullsjö, made of the emigrants from Ryfors, complete with excerpts from the church census in Göteborg's county archives (Nykyrka church archive series A), I have also come to know of these and many more who left this region; a record which is in safe keeping with him and which was of great value to me.

Klas Adolf Knut Ljungström from Björkäng, who emigrated in 1897, was the son of the noted priest, Clas Johan Ljungström, and a versatile person.

The housekeeper, Julia Fröding emigrated on April 1, 1861 from Bredared, originated at Sandhem, and she became a servant in Chicago.

Jenny Lovisa Toll in Bosebygd is shown as a servant in the occupation list. She was employed by the blacksmith family Toll.

The Larssons in Bredared were sons of the patron Larsson of Bredared. Adam and his wife were there as early as 1852. He had "sat in prison one year for arson."

From Broberg we also have Hilma Maria Karlsdotter entered but she changed her mind at the last minute.

The people in Bäckebostugan furnished the earliest emigrants. The farm worker Carl Fredrik Forsberg, born 1823 in Seglora, emigrated subsequently around 1852. The cottage was torn down when the Falköping-Jönköping railroad was built.

The tenant farmers Lager from Fåragömman in Ekeled departed but one brother, Claes, stayed home. The tenant holding Berget seems to have disappeared.

The spruce cottage, according to tradition, would have been built as early as the 15th century. Gylgeryd was a very small farm. Gålleryd would be classified as a factory. Enebacken was a tenant holding under the church in Nykyrke, from which the journeyman tailor, Enström emigrated.

Thorulf Sandén of Hofmantorp, born 1874 in Skövde, and who emigrated in 1895, was considered very skillful in doing different kinds of woodwork. He came back from Chicago after a stay there.

After Carl Levin Brunskog, moved to America Mobacken went to ruin. The Engströms of Maholm on Lake Stråken tanned leather and developed into other manufactures. They were among the earlier emigrants, Fritiof in 1869 and Alexander in 1870. In a similar way the painter A. G. Andersson was possessed of professional knowledge and could continue with his painting on the other side of the Atlantic.

Among those who also emigrated from Ryfors in 1889 were Ivar Viktor Zelander, born 1868, who was particularly well known as the son of the factory administrator and should have had his future secured at home in the factory, but his emigration was owing to a dispute with the guardians of the Sagers' sons.

Also from Ryfors were the Pullman travelers, Åkerbergs, Hurtigs, and Hellströms in particular. In the persons index are to be found, however, two Åkerbergs, and three Hurtigs, but ten Hellströms. They are later shown at Sörarps kvarn, but through other sources we know they are really shown to be from Ryfors.

Moreover, Åke Axell met Karl Hurtig in 1960 in Chicago. Hurtig, who was a brilliant mechanic and was extremely proud of Pullman, started Axell at this trade. He also knew that some of the early emigrants had worked together on the Falköping-Jönköping railroad that ran through the Mullsjö region in the early 1860 decade.

The farm hand Anders Johan Karlsson of the holding Spångerna left in 1893, but returned after two years. The Utterbergs of Utterhaga eventually belonged to Axell's family "brother to my brother-in-law." J. A. Utterberg, born in 1886, became a bartender in Chicago.

The soldier, Sven Pettersson of Bro, in 1878 lived on the holding Broberg, which had stood vacant several years, with his wife Eva Johansdotter and his son, Carl Johan Bro, born in 1848, and his daughter, Inga Maria, born in 1850.

Carl Johan left home in November, 1871 and became a farm hand at Ryfors, where he found a housemaid who took a fancy to him. Love resulted and a wedding was celebrated in May, 1877. Presumably they had a temporary dwelling with Carl Johan's parents at Broberg. After a half year they were able to move to their own home on the holding Nolebo under Margreteholm and here the child Hilma Maria was born in 1878, and Axel Einar in 1880. Carl Johan was now called smith worker and his reading in the book and by heart was represented as considerable.

In the fall of 1881 the pair moved home to Broberg, where the aged parents still lived. Here three more children came into the world: Ellen Kristina in 1882, Beda Linnea, in 1885, and Ernst Vilger on March 26, 1888.

The economic conditions in the home must have looked very meager. The Ryfors factory had had several bad years and they began to talk of the earning possibilities in that "big country in the West." The blacksmith's son, Per Aron Schulz had already emigrated from Ryfors, and perhaps his first letter home would convey news of the good wages "over there." In short, the laborer Carl Bro was granted government permission to undertake his trip to America "without the opportunity to take his wife and children along," and had evidently hurried to come, for he left as early as March 3rd, three weeks before his youngest child would come into the world.

Now it was necessary for the remaining family to move in with the father. Apparently, some insufficient travel money came in letters home to the family, so she therefore applied to the government agency with a request for help "seeing that she herself could not produce sufficient means for such a trip." But the agency decided to open the question, "to reliable prospects of letters for passage of her and the children to come from the husband."

But no money came from either quarter and the wife began finally to give up hope of a happy future in the USA. However, the eldest daughter, Hilma Maria Bro, as a thirteen-year-old, got the chance to come over to the father in 1891.

Necessity smiled, however, at the wife and children living at home, and at her request, the government commission granted 10 kronor to her relief. The wife Augusta made yet another desperate attempt to persuade the ruling body to grant her money for a ticket to America. She renewed her pleas to the commission for ticket money but the answer was cold and chilling: "The wife Augusta Bro had petitioned for a subsidy for a trip to America, but the court cannot grant it, since no assurance can be found that she with her family would be met at disembarkation and since they would be without any means of subsistence in the early part of their stay in America." However, it was ordered that the committee and the director of the needy will seek to place the eldest son "in the most advantageous situation." The decision was changed then so that Augusta would be granted 12 kronor for the eldest son's upkeep from May to October.

The subsequent fate of Augusta is unknown. Was she finally able to get to America or did she die in poverty with an unfulfilled dream of the land of the future?

Karl Alfred Ragnar, son of the soldier Gustaf Ragnar, who was married to Johanna Svensdotter, emigrated to the USA in 1887 but returned in a few years, after earning sufficient money to devote himself to the lumber business and the purchase of a farm. In 1869 he acquired Margreteholm from Johan Gullander for 65,000 kronor. Margreteholm was sold after Alfred's death to Leo Sager in 1914.

Ivar Victor Zelander, born in 1868 in Mora, was the son of the factory manager Johan Victor Zelander and his wife Augusta Mathilda, born Flygelholm. The father succeeded P. V. Eiserman as manager, who left Ryfors after a dispute with the guardians of Sager's sons. The father died in 1894 and was succeeded in his turn by Gustaf Albert Brissman. Ivar Victor emigrated in 1889.

The tailor, Johannes Gustafsson Severin was born in 1843 in Bottnaryd, married in 1867 to Johanna Elisabeth Schultz, born in 1842 in Nykyrke. She was the daughter of Jacob Schultz, who was married to Anna Greta Osbeck. Gustaf emigrated in 1899 together with his wife and four children.

Karl Robert Severin, born 09/22/1869 and his brother, Gustaf Wilhelm, born 07/30/1872 were the sons of the tailor, Johannes Gustafsson Severin. The brothers emigrated to the USA in 1889.

Helfrida Anna Elisabeth Södergren, born in 1882 in Svennered, was the daughter of the smith, Karl Oscar Södergren and his wife Anna Sofia Jansdotter. She emigrated to the USA in 1900.

The smith, Karl Gustaf Forsberg, was born in 1842 in Örebro. The wife's name was Stina Lovisa Persdotter. They had five children. The family emigrated in 1893. Earlier a Forsberg had already traveled westward in 1890, also from Ryfors, namely the forge worker Carl Ulrik Forsberg.

Another who traveled from Ryfors was the forge worker Edvard Landerholm, born in 1860 in Stora Malm, with his wife, Johanna Sträng and three children in the year 1893.

Gerda Sofia Södergren, born in 1885, sister of the earlier named Helfrida Södergren, emigrated in 1901.

August Henrik Hurtig, born in 1884, was the son of pencil maker Johan August Hurtig, married to Lisa Johansdotter. August emigrated in 1901

The brother Karl Reinhold Hurtig, born in 1888 emigrated in 1906 and got work at "the big Pullman factory in Chicago."

Frans Augustsson, born 01/30/1875, was the son of the miller August Jönsson and his wife Anna Stina Johansdotter. They emigrated to the USA in 1900.

Thanks to common handiness and definite experience in carpentry many found employment in Pullman's carpenter shops, where they were effective for a long time. The question of dwellings was answered without great difficulty because the housing was in the town of Pullman.

Earlier we have followed one of these Pullman carpenters from Ryfors, Ernst Åkerberg, from 1902 to 1905 with a continuation farther on in the book between 1906 and 1954 in Chapter 8.

For the most part we also know now how it went with the first Hellström. Johan Wilhelm, ended up at Pullman in 1881 when the town was built.

The contrast must have seemed strong for him and the others when they came from the peacefulness of the shady green ridges around Stråken's blue waters to the flat landscape around Pullman with its many factory chimneys and its proximity to the big city's rapid pulse.

The emigration west of Lake Vättern

If one wished to seek an answer to the *question*, how great the emigration really was from the region west of Vättern, the information is to be found with Gustaf Sundbärg in the *Emigration Report 1881-1900*, Appendix V. The cities of Jönköping, Tidaholm, and Falköping had in the strength of their large populations the greatest number of emigrants. Among the parishes, Sandhem, Habo, Gustav Adolf, and Hössna can be pointed out, all with more than 300 persons bound for America. Nykyrke with Mullsjö had 134.

The small cities, Ulricehamn, Tidaholm and Falköping were without industries of significance and the factories in the region were affected periodically by poor economic conditions and with the dismissals that resulted. The industries in Jönköping, Huskvarna, and Norrahammar had undergone such expansion that the emigrations were curtailed at times in their region.

Conditions in Jönköping's region could influence the situation only to a limited extent at Hökensås and the Mullsjö-Sandhem region.

Eric De Geer, who, in a survey in *Ymer*, 1959, has dealt with the West Swedish emigration, amplified this in a letter to the author, 02/18/1998, drawing the conclusion that the emigrations in this actual region were due to its becoming stagnated and lying remote from the expanding center.

Göteborg's field of influence didn't reach these regions, nor did Borås' textile based expansion. Therefore the information about employment possibilities in Göteborg and Stockholm didn't reach them. However, information about the great land of opportunity came, effectively enough, from practically everywhere, and for the lack of an obvious alternative the choice was America for so many.

The regions and the new times

To an earlier question about the region's general character, I can reply by citing what I wrote in Smålands culture sketches 1962, in an article about, "Sensitivity to the New Ideas." Calculated from east to west I showed that Bankeryd in Jönköping's county appeared early with innovation of a different kind. The vicinity of Jönköping played a clearly decisive roll. Habo and Sandhem, however, were significantly behind. Here, for example, a prominent craft region could often be characterized as a manufacturer of kitchen utensils. Within Gustav Adolf's parish there was still a considerable difference between the newly emerged church village on the one side and the timber tracts situated in the western part of the parish on the other. In all cases the west coast region of Lake Vättern was free of middle-Swedish traits regarding older building techniques. Willingness to accept the new was therefore noticeable in the southern Vättern region where I cited examples in the electric lights installed in many places in Tveta diocese during the 1890 decade, sewing machines around 1880, and separators in 1895. The marks of modernization in Nykyrke definitely took hold when the Jönköping-Falköping railroad was run past Mullsjö and the region reached larger and more distant markets. In particular, the earnings from timber sales to England increased. In this connection Ryfors, with its iron works, its nail and iron rod forges, and its sawmills, had taken a prominent place. As an example it can be stated that forging at Ryfors was first carried out with the so-called German hearth, but in the 1860 decade it was changed to the Franche-Comté method for the manufacture of horse shoes, harrows, nails, axes, and much more. Water power came to be used later in regions where rapids supplied the demands for electrical energy, continuing until the 1930 decade.

I have lately analyzed the typical and separate region just southwest of this place in the book, *Buildings on the horse paths of the year, 1000 around Åsunden,* 1997, page 179ff.

By way of conclusion; to the expressiveness of the vast forests and the long-stretching Lake Stråken with its extension into the Tidan, belongs also the responsibility for their care; not the least, of preserving older buildings like the manor houses of upper Ryfors, lower Ryfors, and of Nääs; the mills and power plants and the iron forge and dairies of Ryfors. Here the Nordic museum made a first inquiry in 1930 and the Västergötland museum made another in 1977 through Eric Juhlin and Bengt Spade. In Juhlin's inventories the structures are rated as to their preserved value. The most outstanding of them would probably be the gate house at Nääs. It stood completed in 1695. The farm was then owned by Berndt Diedric Mörner, Colonel and commander of Jönköpings regiment. In an article in *Västergötlands Society of Antiquities Magazine* of 1996 the present owner of Nääs, Lars Ågren has assumed that the knot timbered and red painted gatehouse at Nääs perhaps is an unknown work of Erik Dahlberg, page 37ff. It can be added in this connection that First Chief Stable Master, Edvard Sager, and his son, John Henry Sager at Ryfors on several occasions authorized the repair of the farm buildings.

It was in the year 1876 that the farm was acquired by Ryfors. The buildings in the characteristic style of Ryfors usually had facades tinted in brown.

The rapids in the watercourse drove the mills, die presses, and power stations. The current in the Tidan is powerful during a great part of the year and it was that which made the location ideal for the blast furnace which was utilized already in 1789.

At my request Tage Åkerberg has kindly written a close-up of what it was like to grow up in the village. It follows here as a supplement to round off this chapter.

Supplement 1 to chapter IV
Growing up in Ryfors

Behind the attic window in Bengt Spade's drawing "Workers' houses at Ryfors Mill" we had our bedroom, and there I was born in 1928 and my brother in 1925. We lived in one room and kitchen on the second floor at the farm and also had a gable room in the attic. In the entrance hall was a pantry, and one came from the hall into the kitchen. The stationary fixtures in the kitchen consisted of a large over-and-under cupboard, a dish stand with space for a sink bucket under it, wood stove, and a bench with a firewood bin. A kitchen settee, two chairs, a stool, a commode, and the obligatory line from wall to wall over the stove for drying wet clothes completed the kitchen's interior.

Within the kitchen was a utility room. There alongside the buckets were the cooking pots and the kitchen utensils on the shelves with the calender and a small wardrobe. As is evident, we had no water or drainpipe. But we had electricity–and yet did not use a stronger lamp than 15 watts. We who remained at the factory lived rent-free with free electricity and firewood. On the whole, all the dwellings had similar arrangements and furnishings and the pattern didn't vary a great deal.

Our house, along with the other houses and with the outbuildings belonging to them, the courtyard, kitchen yard, potato field, formed a community unit which is called improperly in common speech, "Bruket" (the factory or mill). Those who lived in upper Ryfors Bruk used either "Bruket" or "herrgår'n" (manor). Later, this was the community name for the dwelling units that lay higher above the manor house. During the years up to about the middle of the 40s decade this was, on the whole, where all eligible inhabitants at Ryfors and the community lived.

It is about this period, this people, and this environment that I will relate my experience.

Throughout the Bruks neighborhood with nearly all the workers and dwellers in the same region, it was natural to be at home across the boundaries of generations. Of the approximate 100 persons who lived in Ryfors at that time, there were 15-20 children. Even within this group we were dealing with the moving boundaries of age, so we were not so many, for understandable reasons.

We children frequented the different work places now and then, sometimes because it was interesting or exciting, sometimes to help, but more often to get help ourselves. We went most often to the forge where Pappa and Luther Franzén worked, first to see if any of the neighborhood's cars were in for overhaul. That meant that we could count on a ride on the test drive later on. But it was also fun to see the shower of sparks when they hammered. It was best when the air hammer was used. The great din made the walls shake.

In the carpenter shop nearby we collected scraps of board to burn in the wood stove. But most often we visited the sites of some of our innumerable boats under construction. Otto Andersson or Werner Nilsson were always to be seen at the bandsaw where they would fashion a keel for us. We went to the corner at the planing bench and fashioned a finished boat and with a bit of sheet metal from the smithy on the keel, it was ready for sailing.

Ivar Pettersson managed the big crew in the cow house. It was always fun to go and hang around among the cows and calves and at a respectful distance watch the big bull that stood and glared and snorted. Grandfather in his time had stood at the cow barn in the morning and "dealt out people" (distributed work). By the cow barn were logs, sheds, and a big wood-pile where wood was chopped for the needs of the manor house. Pappa worked there in his youth together with an old tenant farmer. I believe it was Edvard of Sprängerna. The tenant farmer also had the task of fetching grain from the manor house kitchen for the French hens.

The big garden was managed by the gardener, Arvid Lind, and several helpers. Arvid and his wife, Signe, had four children and a very hospitable home. There was naturally an advantage in being cronies with the gardener's kids: the garden and its abundance stood pretty much at our disposition. There was, like in the garden of Eden, a tree with forbidden fruit, an apple tree which was 100% reserved for the Chief Stable Master, Edvard Sager, and we absolutely did not mix with him, nor he with us. That bum occasionally came to Ryfors and usually spent the night in the fire pit in the greenhouse.

Karl Jönsson, "Jösskarl" or "Jösse" came every year to do the grinding in Ryfors mill. It was exciting to visit "Jösse" in the half-darkness of the mill and to hear the sound of the water wheel turning the wood-cogged wheel and axle, and the stones' monotonous grind. When the work demanded he would sleep over in the mill room. When "Jösse" ground our rye, he and his sister "Jöss Anna", with whom he lived, were always well-fed.

At the lower falls lay the Lower Ryfors power house which in the beginning of the 30s-decade was run by the Hellströms. Now Gustav Hellström was responsible for the production and distribution of electricity from the power station. Gustav was cheerful and humorous and had much fun with we children. They lived in the family home in Sörarp, whence eleven children emigrated to America and only one, Gustaf's father Pontus, returned.

Under the gables of the big granary at the mill/power station was the office, a branch of Ljungqvist's successors in Mullsjö. The office, a genuine country store and simply called "boa," was an important place at Ryfors. The warden was Bror Spång. He was nice to we children and we utilized his goodness to the full. He supplied us with big corrugated cardboard cartons and wooden boxes to play with. In winter, when timber was hauled down to the sawmill below, or when some peasant came with horse and sled, we asked "Bror" for binding twine. We would tie it firmly to our sleds and get a free ride all the way to Blandebacka. Coming back we would have a kilometer-long downward slope.

In the afternoons the newspaper and mail bag came from Mullsjö. In their leisure time the committee gathered there for a chat. There was one chair in the office and it was usually occupied by the driver Eriksson. He had the habit of emphasizing his argument by striking his spiked cane against the floor, thus leaving an indelible memory in the wood floor after him. Most of the trade was "on the books" and not in direct payment. Many farmers and tenant farmers had butter with them as part payment in trade. The butter usually came in the form of a lump wrapped in paper, or for lack of that, on paper in a towel. Many farms and places around Ryfors still had no electricity. Therefore kerosene always stood on the price list.

When school ended in summer the "Stockholmers" came. That was before all the children and grandchildren of Robert Hurtig and Levin Holm visited Ryfors for the summer weeks. Then the big courtyard became the village gathering place and activity center. The whole summer a croquet game was set up in the area and young and old played together daily. We often heard Uncle Robert Hurtig when he approached and came in through the gate by our house. Although born in 1857 he was still as hale as a youngster. He was supervisor of the Övres power station and of the eel traps at the falls. In summer he walked in galoshes without shoes, and it was that flapping sound of the loose boots that we heard. He was an eager fisherman and he competed the most and longest with his friend and rival-brother, the gardener.

Every afternoon in summer we swam. It was a happy group of children as, under Aunt "Fiffi's" guidance and responsibility, we moved through the forest to the swimming place at Stråken. We did not really swim all day. When the blueberries ripened we had in our thoughts the heavy obligation to pluck the winter's requisite of berries.

In the evenings we often went for a walk together. The possibilities were many along the wood's fine path. We walked to "Twelve Stones," to Kärleksudden, to Pinnabron, or perhaps even to Fröjered's summer house. The love of nature was rooted in us in this way.

Since we lived in the country we followed the times and events of the year. In spring we picked blue anemone, white anemone, and lily of the valley. When the bird cherry bloomed that was the day for white fish and later we fished in the lake from a boat. We dug up turnips. There was no coercion but we were expected to produce. We got ½ öre [penny] per armful and perhaps some öre in addition for good thinning out. In mid-summer there was a gathering at the manor house around the maypole with coffee, dance, and games. The other traditional holiday was when the harvest was gathered in. When the feast was offered it was on gigantic wheat buns and sandwiches of fresh baked rye bread with thick cheese slices. Here fresh-brewed beer was drunk. Often, when the feast was held in the picture theater, the village orchestra would also play.

Sometimes we were invited to the Countess Marie Sager's. I have a pleasant memory of a birthday party in the upper floor in what is today called Black Cottage, then simply–the countess'. In the room were four door openings with only two doors. The other two had mirrors that completely filled the door frames. During the welcoming ceremony Konrad of Granbäck came in front of one of the mirrors and discovered that he still had scarcely greeted half of the guests. With the words, "Well, I never! What strange people we have here," he stretched his hand towards his own reflection. Laughter and applause!

I remember in 1937 when David Hillstrom with his wife, Clara and their eldest son, Armour, came from America. It was a summer with many coffee invitations. One time outside the office I got a 1-krona coin from him; it was just as much as Pappa's hourly wage. When the day came for their return journey, many stood at the stone gate to take farewell, some of them he was seeing for the last time. When the car with the Americans disappeared, a part of us went to Spängerna to wave when the train to Göteborg passed over the Stråken bridge. My uncle Ernst wrote, when he returned from his visit to Sweden in 1912 of a corresponding situation: "I saw Pappa and Mia first at Spängerna. The feeling that came over me cannot be written in words"!

Later, during 1937, Robert Hurtig died at age 80. Before burial the casket stood at a bier made of a wood frame and covered with twigs. It was placed in the garden at the lilac bushes along the walls between the dwelling houses. I also remember grandmother's casket in the same place. And I especially remember Mamma's white casket. She died when I was four years old.

After Chief Stable Master Edvard Sager's death in 1939 and the son, John Henry's succession, things continued mostly in the usual way in the beginning. The sounds of the Chief Stable Master's trips with horse and buggy to and from Mullsjö disappeared but not right away, of course. The substitute was a silent tandem bicycle. The first new trustee that took over gave Pappa, at any rate, a certain expectation. He had the ability to find a new work opportunity but cooperation with John Henry Sager collapsed. However, in that defunct dairy a laundry was established by an enterprising person in just a few years. By that time I had gone into the secondary school in Jönköping and one day a teacher, an old bachelor, came to me and said that he made use of Ryfors laundry. He never had such fine clean shirts. That was not so strange because the work was performed by an expert, the Chief Stable Master's old lady who gloss-ironed and held that position at the laundry.

The next trustee had the well-known qualifications that he had been an elephant hunter in Africa. He got a horse and was able to come riding into the farm and from horseback with strident voice shouted to the people in the houses. He too, moved, and became an auctioneer at the live animal auctions in Jönköping. There his vocal resources served him better.

There came several other trustees but developments went in a negative direction. Numerous dwellings stood empty. The elders died and the others moved from Ryfors. The work for the remaining became all the more meaningless. Even Pappa considered moving from Ryfors but he never needed to make that decision. He died during the snowy winter of 1951 in a work accident in connection with an old telephone line that was about to be taken down. Even that was meaningless work.

To conclude my story a little more positively, I will quote Doris Selander, Levin Holms' youngest daughter, who lived next door to me during my student years in Borås. She had also left her heart in Ryfors and always said when I rode home over the holidays: "Don't forget to say hello to the forest"!

---

[1] *Thou Ancient, Thou Free.*

From Vera and Leo Sager's visit to Chicago; a great day for the Ryfors-born. Vera and Leo Sager lived at Ryfors and at Stockholm. Vera Sager was called "Gracious Lady" and was addressed by ordinary people as, "Your Grace." Her home in Stockholm finally became the Prime Minister's residence after she died. David Hillstrom sits to the left at Vera Sager's side. Photo owned by Armour Hillstrom.

Taken in early 1920 decade. Seated in the front row are all the Hillstrom brothers who emigrated to America: Johan, Edward, Reinhold, Fingal, Fritiof, David and Phillip. In the back row: brother-in-law, Ernst Åkerberg, Johan's three sons and two sons-in-law to Edward. Photo owned by Armour Hillstrom.

Robert Sager makes a speech to the village tenants on the steps of the corn exchange in the year 1908, presumably on the occasion of the 50-year anniversary of his father's death.
From B. Berglund, Ryfors Bruk, 1742-1920, page 146.

Main building of Ryfors village or "Ryfors Svarta" [black]. The building was moved, presumably in the year 1823, from Gunillaberg in Bottnaryd, but owes its present appearance to the extensive modernization in the 1880 decade. The three drawings are by Bengt Spade and are used by permission of the artist.

Ryds mill

Lower Ryfors power station. Here Sörarps mill was located earlier.

Workers' residences at Ryfors. On the second floor to the right, Tage Åkerberg grew up. Drawing by Bengt Spade.

Chapter V
The Town of Pullman
"Villages of Vision"

In the introduction I have already put the *question* of why George Mortimer Pullman established an ideal town for his workers. He could, of course, have been just as easily satisfied with building the traditional dreary town with factories and houses "straight up and down" after he had cleared out the newly acquired swamp area along Lake Calumet.

Had there been anything like it before in America? Had he heard that there was any such thing in Europe? For such towns were certainly there. Outside Delft in Holland, for example, the Van Markens town, Agneta, had been built.

In her book, *Villages of Vision,* 1975, Gillian Darley writes the following about Agneta, page 145.

> Here in 1883 the yeast and vegetable oil concern had founded a ten-acre park of cottages for their workers, grouped around a circular road with a lake in the middle. Eighty families were housed here, and together with traditional-style cottages went numerous small thoughtful details such as wooden rubbish boxes and special clothes horses for outside airing of clothes. The motto at the works was 'the factory for all; all for the factory,' and the general scheme was far more cooperative than anything else ever set up. The housing was owned by the Common Property Society and the aim was to keep an air of self-determination throughout.

Darley talks further about Bournville in Warwickshire, Port Sunlight in Cheshire, Moravian village at Manchester, Bedford Park, London, and Krupp's Margaretenhöhe in the Ruhr region among others, but she does not go into the situation regarding the planning of the town of Pullman. She dates it in the late 1880s, but there she is wrong. The town of Pullman began to be built in 1880-1882. Turning to S. Buder, 1967, p. 146, we read as follows:

> Pullman, the most ambitious of American foundations built in the 1880s, was gripped by a desperate strike in 1894, and behind the facade of a model settlement were found hidden the skeletons of a truly appalling situation where the workers were suffering more than many who lived in unambitious tenement communities elsewhere.

A few other works that might possibly answer my *questions* are Dolores Hayden's *Seven American Utopias*, 1976, and Helen Rosenau's *The Ideal City,* 1959.

The seven American towns are the Shakers of Hancock, Massachusetts, the Mormons of Nauvoo, Illinois, the Fourierists of Phalanx, New Jersey, the Perfectionists of Oneida, New York, the Inspirationists of Amana, Iowa, the Union Colonists of Greeley, Colorado, and the Cooperative Colonists of Llano del Rio, California.

The town of Pullman is not to be found among these seven American utopias. Dolores Hayden's selections appear to be primarily based on architecture, and are developed from idealistic cultural values. One of the many architects, however, had been inspired by Pullman. It was Alice Constance Austin, creator of Llano del Rio. She had become acquainted with the model town of Pullman while at the Columbian Exposition of 1893 and thereafter resolved to study design and architecture.

Helen Rosenau, lecturer in Art History at Manchester University, lays her main stress on the concepts and thoughts about the early ideal towns during the renaissance and baroque periods.

Pullman's own architect, Solon Spencer Beman, gradually became a famous man. As early as 1879 he was commissioned to draw up the guidelines for the town of Pullman and he put forth ideas to his commission giver on what form the factories and dwellings would take. Early on, he is seen to be concentrating on a utopian design and preferring to work in the Romanesque or Queen Anne style.

> He trained in the office of Richard Upjohn, the leading ecclesiological architect of the mid- nineteenth century. After leaving the firm, he won a prestigious commission in 1879 from George Pullman, the railroad magnate, to develop his company town on the shore of Lake Calumet, south of Chicago. Beman created the town as a moral statement, a utopia established to insure the morality and efficiency of its residents. His design of the 'noble experiment' at Pullman made him famous. During the 1880s and the 1890s he built a number of office buildings in Milwaukee and Chicago.

From Chicago History, 1994, p. 21

A contemporaneous report of the towns is given in an article in *The New Illustrated Times* of February 14, 1885, no. 7, page 56ff. It is titled "Workers' Communities Abroad", and points out that these are really nothing new or remarkable.

The article's author thinks it was the successful creation of the comfortable sleeping cars by Pullman that made the erection of large new buildings for their construction a necessity. It was then he had the occasion to realize "a cherished idea" he had long held. He wanted above all

> ...to protect his tenants from the night perils of the big cities. He convinced himself that the execution of his idea did not have anything but financial difficulties to contend with, and he was certain that it would depend on external circumstance if mankind's healthy nature could prevail over its evil inclination.

> Those workers in overpopulated towns are seldom as healthy or happy as they should be, so Mr. Pullman would prepare them to develop their natural ability. He would build an ideal town for his workers. Said and done.

This article was written when the town was four years old, and it describes the actual situation with the hotel, homes, school, stables, bank, library, telegraph office, post office, theater, church, and much more.

It is most likely, however, that Pullman himself had the decisive impulse to build an ideal town when he visited Saltaire in Yorkshire. Gillian Darley gives us this information about the town, 1975, p.146.

> Saltaire: Generally recognized as the first industrial model village and certainly the most ambitious, was supposedly inspired by Disraeli's novel, *Sybil*, 1845, which has a description of Trafford's factory village. Architects for Sir Titus Salt were Lockwood and Mawson (of Bradford). Planned on a grid, housing was Italianate with variation between 2 and 3 storeys; the factory, also Italianate; institute, almshouses, park, steam laundry–all serving workers in alpaca worsted. Founded in 1850, by 1872 there were 820 houses.

Darley also shows a picture from Saltaire with its Congregational Church between the house rows, p. 64.

> Cottage terraces at Saltaire with the Congregational Church in the distance. The housing has more than basic detailing (such as the arched window surrounds) and the lines are broken by the interposition of three-storeyed housing at intervals. Small yards are provided, and although the houses are back to back, there is still a refreshing view of the open country beyond.

In his book, *The Pullman Strike, The Story of a Unique Experiment and of a Great Labor Upheaval*, 1964, Almont Lindsey also lets us know that Pullman, during a European trip in 1873, visited three model towns of the paternalistic pattern: Saltaire, England; Guise, France; and Essen, Germany. "It is not known to what extent, if at all, George Pullman borrowed from them, but he was doubtless familiar with their existence from the publicity they received during the seventies and eighties," p. 33.

Thomas Grant, quoting Lindsey from an article in *American Journal of Politics,* V, 1894, p. 199, goes even further and declares: "Pullman used Saltaire as a model for imitation and followed it very closely."

Sir Titus Salt built the 1853 houses of stone for his 4000 textile workers in Saltaire in the vicinity of Bradford, all surrounded with rows of trees, lawns and flower beds, parks, sports arenas, and bath facilities. There was also a church in the Italian style, schools, offices, and a recreation center. The workers should have felt good physically and mentally, but it was Sir Titus Salt who controlled everything. In one regard he was more foresighted than his followers were. "He was willing to sell lots upon which operatives could build their homes," p. 34.

In spite of all the careful planning, however, the town of Pullman did not prosper very long. The man behind the town, George Mortimer Pullman had, of course, died at the age of 66 on the 19th of October, 1897. After the great strike of 1894 the Supreme Court, through an 1898 decision, forced the Pullman Company to sell its non-industrial property, and its private property was to be separated according to the factory's contract with Chicago; the main office was to be moved, and everything concentrated in Pullman town.

By the end of 1907 the Pullman Company had sold most of its shares in its own Pullman town. Changes in the traditional production methods in the workshops meant that wood was no longer needed to such a great extent since steel production had become prevalent. The result was that our Swedish wood craftsmen gradually began to face unemployment. In some cases they were not retrained.

We have been following the Swedish Elim congregation up to the beginning of the 1930s. The Swedes had, of course, established themselves in large numbers, but as the North Europeans began to move out of the town of Pullman in the 1920s, the South and East Europeans moved in.

"Historic Pullman Foundation" an institution for preservation

Toward the end of the 1950 decade, a concern for the area arose when a local business organization forged a plan to tear down part of the Pullman community. But then the inhabitants began a strong reaction; gathered, and created the Pullman Civic Organization (PCO). Some of them had come to realize that if people got together and formed an organization, perhaps they could save the town and its many unique buildings from being bought up and torn down. Those concerned brought their ideas to the City of Chicago, the State of Illinois, and the whole country, and it succeeded gradually. Consequently in 1969 they received landmark status from the State of Illinois, a recognition that this really was a community worth investing in.[1]

In 1973, The Historic Pullman Foundation, (HPF), was formed, a separate group from PCO. All the more wind in the sails. Ever since, the foundation has created different types of activities in the town's life, established Pullman's visitors' center, and privately purchased the most valuable buildings: The Hotel Florence, Market Hall, the Pullman Historic Center, and many more. In 1991, the State of Illinois purchased the clock tower and the Hotel Florence.[2]

Plans for a railroad museum began to take form and the cultural reserve was expanded. The town of Pullman has again become a community with people who preserve the past in a living present.

A newsletter, *Update: Historic Pullman,* comes out regularly. Through this newsletter of the Historic Pullman Foundation we can know how the work progresses.

Remarkably enough, the majority of the factory buildings are still there. "Not used for anything, they have not been torn down, probably because the property is under protection of the Illinois Historic Preservation Agency." It adds by way of information, "It would be expensive to raze them unless the property was put to some profitable use."

In the opening chapter I have already mentioned my own interest in the town of Pullman, its advent as a model community, and its continuous refurbishing. Therefore I go back partly to my own impressions, and partly I am led to draw parallels with Klippan in Göteborg and with Jonsered close by Göteborg; and I now continue the chapter with these.

Comparative perspective
Klippan

A characteristic of Klippan was also the paternalistic management of the factory. It too expressed itself in an extensive social activity. Over and above the factory and a porter brewery, the dwellings for the workers provided nearly everything relating to the necessities of living within the region; church, priest, school, food store, bakery, and bath house.

The brick dwelling structures were built here in 1856-58, Klippangatan 14-20 [Address]. They were intended for 10 to 18 households. The architect was the well-known A. W. Edelsvärd. From the 1860s, according to existing information, the rent for a room, kitchen, pantry, woodshed, part of an attic, amounted to 5½ riksdaler per month. Fire insurance premiums, even for the workers' personal property, were paid by the factory management. The Scotsman, David Carnegie Jr. regarded the role of the factory's leader as having responsibility for the health of his workers' "body and soul." The chapel became a direct link between Göteborg and Scotland, in that Carnegie arranged to build a chapel nearly identical to the one in his home village, Balquidder. It is built in the English Gothic style, having a little bell tower on the gable and is named after St.Brigit, an Irish-Scottish saint.

The industrial region of Klippan has an intrinsic tradition from the 18th Century; the preserved buildings show an advanced construction development for their time, and the housing areas from the beginning of the 1880 decade up to modern times have strong social and architectural historic value.

The original industry was the production of crockery and glass, and after 1808 a sugar mill and a porter brewery were established by A. R. Lorent. In 1813 he installed one of the first steam engines in Sweden. In 1836 the Lorent factories were taken over by David Carnegie Jr.

The Klippan region, as well as the town of Pullman, demonstrates how, during the 19th Century, some of the industrial leaders, in a philanthropic spirit, tried to improve their workers' living relationships by building model establishments.

Therefore parallels exist here; with David Carnegie Jr. and his closest assistant, Oscar Ekman, in Klippan near Göteborg, and with George Mortimer Pullman in the town of Pullman near Chicago; who cared for their workers with a socio-religious ardor through row arrangements of dwellings alongside industrial constructions.

Jonsered

In Jonsered, another parallel, the factory leadership also took early responsibility for such establishments as schools, churches, nursing, food service, shops, etc. The first buildings lay in the factory area and were built of wood. They were followed by long two-story row houses of brick after the Scottish pattern, a strict empire architecture, placed facing the country road with thought given to the frontages. The factory buildings were one-story with roofs of the saw-tooth type and the floors covered with poured stone from Kinnekulle. In some respects these dwellings are like those settings in Klippan, where civil servants' villas are surrounded with gardens.

The motive force behind the Gibson family's social work alludes ultimately to Jonsered, to Carnegie's Klippan, and to Pullman's town, holding on to the skillful and reliable workers who could run the enterprise at reasonable wages. William Gibson (I) was born in Scotland in 1783, emigrated to Göteborg at the age of 14. There he began the trade of rope-making, linen-weaving, and foundry work in Majorna. In 1834, together with the Scot, Alexander Keiller, he purchased Jonsered, where factories had been vacated. Under his leadership (died 1857), and that of his son, William G. (II) (1816-1865), and his grandson, William G. (III) (1848-1917), the industry at Jonsered became "an enterprise of considerable proportions." *Norse Family Book,* 1954, p.910. Like Carnegie and Pullman, the Gibsons were generally very important to their area. For example, thanks to their assistance, the railroad connection Göteborg-Jonsered came in 1865; also the first telegraph line for industrial use, and much more.

Industries in Jonsered were, from the beginning in 1832, based on sail cloth weaving and on textiles. Cotton spinning and weaving came in 1844-1855.

The floor plans of the worker's dwellings at Jonsered and Klippan provided only one room and kitchen, while those in the town of Pullman might include up to four rooms and a kitchen. When the free-standing workers' homes in the jugend style were erected, it meant that they could compete with the free-standing workers' homes in the town of Pullman, even though Pullman was a step ahead because of its sanitary equipment.

Ingrid Mesterton's detailed writings on Swedish cities in 1953 included a study of Jonsered as a community. She established that furnishings in the early workers' towns consisted of a board table, some straight chairs, a pull-out sofa, and a table bench for children. As storage furniture they used a draw chest and a corner cupboard. Often the furniture was painted in a red or brown color. A wall clock was a luxury article, but with some pictures or little tables, or a work box, furnishings were complete. Among the personal possessions were glassware, copper-ware, coffee pot, saucepans, candle sticks, etc. One had to fetch water for cooking and washing from far away at the Säve creek.

A similarity between Jonsered and the town of Pullman also appears in the form of a nearby "residents' garden" from which produce was made available to the factory and work area households. Another was that the main office lay outside the work area; Göteborg in Gibson's case and Chicago in Pullman's. A third similarity was that the owners' homes were model edifices; in Jonsered on a hill with a view over Lake Aspen; in the town of Pullman and in Klippan, in expensive isolation. A fourth was that the communities produced good sportsmen. This was particularly true, as we have seen earlier, in the town of Pullman with its cricket and baseball teams. Thanks to the British influence in Jonsered, and to the fact that Great Britain had been a pioneer in the area of sports, we may surmise that sports training began early in Jonsered. It got its start with the youth societies in 1892, the Gymnastic and Sports Society in 1903, and the Sports Society in 1921. The most distinguished football players are believed to be Erik Börjesson, Konrad Törnqvist, John Olson, Lindoff Andersson, and Gunnar Zacharoff. In the field of athletics Bokedalen had good runners and running broad jumpers. Jonsered's factories gave yearly support to these activities; see *The Books of Jonsered,* 1982.

> Differences between worker's and official's living styles in Jonsered relating to corresponding conditions in similar communities was the object of a study by Birgitta Skarin Frykman, *Food and Meals Among Workers and Officials in Jonsered During the 1900 Decade,* 1976. She establishes there that the workers often had a meal late in the day while the officials, usually ate at two. The higher officials normally brought in traditions from their level of origin. They adopted innovations sooner than their workers, such as tomatoes and unsweetened bread. They also had, naturally enough, less trouble in availing themselves of credit in the purchase of food products. To a greater extent than the workers, they got food sent home from the stores. An improved economy gradually influenced the workers' trade position in such a way that their own agriculture diminished in importance. The employment of women and the increased distance to the workplace resulted in later effects on the character of meals
>
> Also within the community were different closed social groups which seemed to be those with whom people first associated. p. 143ff.

Jonsered, similar to Klippan and the town of Pullman, was therefore a closed community. The pattern had certainly been drawn from Scotland and England. Ingrid Mesterton has not, so far as is known, directly named an architect or architects of the constructions in Jonsered. The high-positioned churches there are designed, like those in Klippan, by A. W. Edelsvärd. Elov Lindälv named him as responsible for Klippan's new constructions in the 1850 decade, verified earlier by Gunilla Linde Bjur; and I have stood by Thomas Grant's belief that Pullman got his idea in the year 1873 in Saltaire, Yorkshire, and later had his architect, Solon Spencer Beman, put it into practice.

To conclude, I want to express my admiration for those who had thoughts of an ideal town; who brought those ideas to formulation and carried them out.

Among noisy factories and roaring machines, the dwelling areas offered workers a refuge from the weekday hardships.

---

[1] In 1969, Pullman received State of Illinois landmark status; South Pullman (the original housing from 111th Street to 115th Street including factories north of 111th Street to 109th Place along Cottage Grove Avenue).

In 1971, the entire Pullman district (103rd Street to 115th Street) received National Registry designation.

In 1972, South Pullman (109th Place to 115th Street, Cottage Grove to Langley) Received City of Chicago landmark status.

Frank Beberdick, *Chicago's Historic Pullman District*, (Charleston SC: Arcadia Publishing, 1998) p. 126

[2] The Clock Tower building was owned by the Pullman company until 1957. It was subsequently bought and sold by several private business interests, mostly for storage space. It was finally purchased by the State of Illinois in 1991 under former Governor Thompson for the proposed Pullman Interpretive Museum. The Clock Tower complex suffered a devastating fire on December 1, 1998. Plans have been made for restoration using public subscription and government funds.

Update: Historic Pullman, Newsletter of the Historic Pullman Foundation, January, 1999.

The architect Solon Spencer Beman. Portrait painted by Oliver Denton Grover for the Illinois chapter of the American Institute of Architects. From Chicago History, 1994, page 21.
Publication of the Chicago Historical Society.

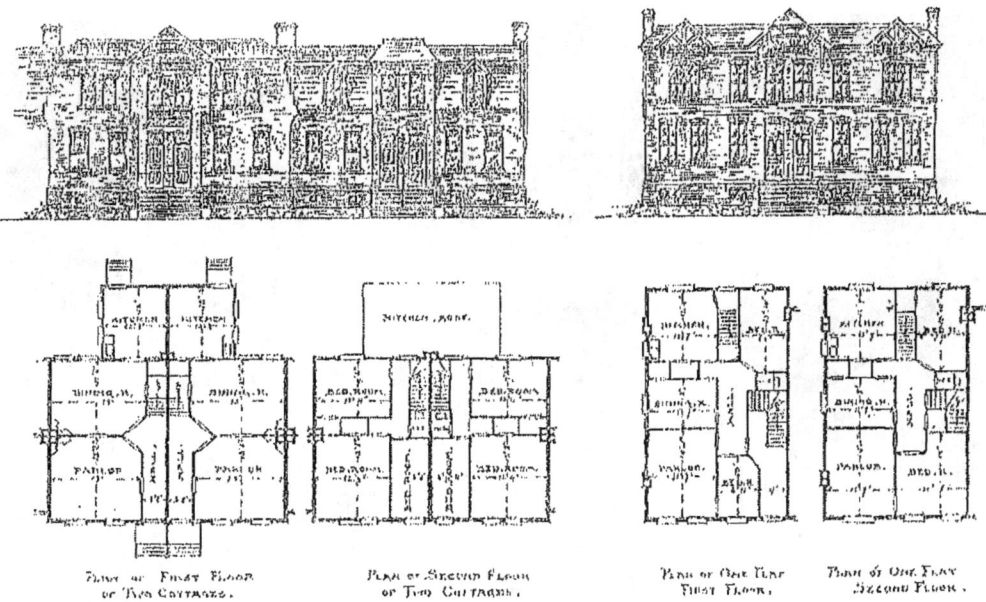

Pullman Homes. Historic Pullman Foundation.

Top left, St. Lawrence Ave. (formerly Watt Ave.), between 112th and 113th Streets. Row houses restored to original condition. Photo by R. E. Johnson.
Top right, North Pullman, 10514 Maryland Ave. Birthplace of Raymond E. Johnson's father, Gust J. Johnson. These row houses await renovation. Photo by R. E. Johnson.

Pullman's Church. Greenstone Church on St. Lawrence, formerly Watt Ave. Photo by R. E. Johnson.

Car shops north of 111th Street. Photo by R. E. Johnson

Workers' homes in the Klippan region. From Linde Bjur, Facades in Goteborg, 1996, p. 43. Photo Hans Hammarskiöld.

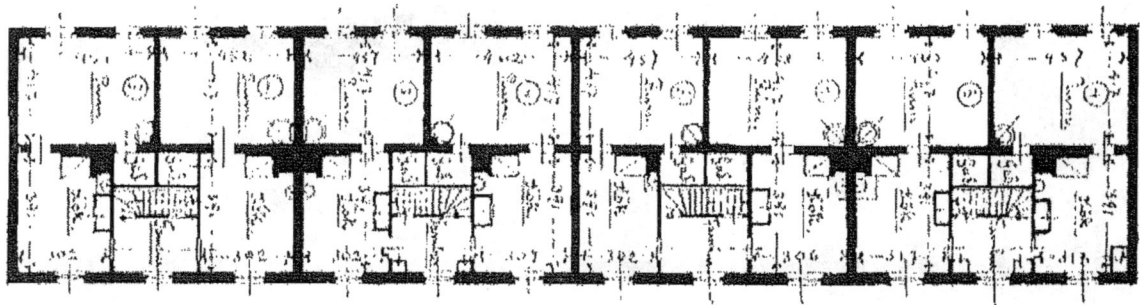

Andra våningen

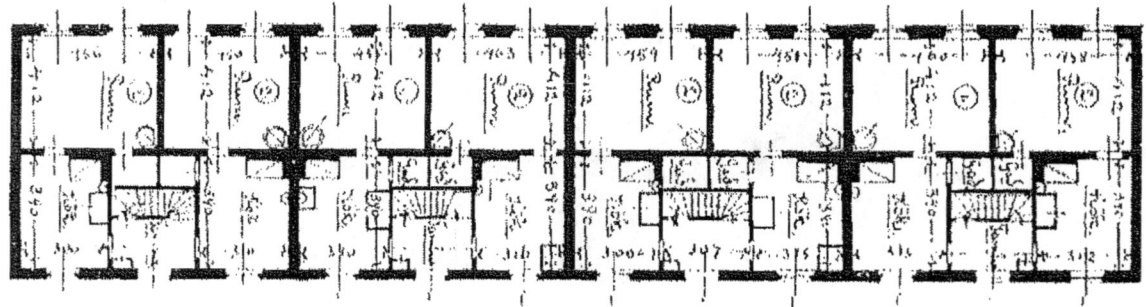

Housing units built of brick. 1856-1858. Architect, A. W. Edelsvard. From Lindalv 1977, page 81. [On the drawing—ground floor, second floor.]

Chapter VI
In the Shadow of the Metropolis

Swedish-American comparisons

In my earlier book about America, the Swedes in New England, particularly in New Britain, CT, 1988, I described the trends and studies made by Swedish ethnologists concentrating on America. With descriptions from my own field studies in America and the observations I made, I realized that I had no ethnological prototype on which to build further, but had to find my own methodology.

In the course of an investigation in New England, certain documents of Swedish cultural manifestations were accordingly chosen from an industrial town for the purpose of making a deep study. The choice fell on New Britain in Connecticut, situated in the shadow of the large city, Hartford. There I examined how life shaped itself for the Swedes.

During a number of in-depth interviews, I put questions about recruiting and profiling, particularly as applied to marriage patterns, baptismal names, the religious community, and society.

The life's experiences, evaluations, and performances of the persons interviewed constituted the most important basic material. I could thereafter compare the realities in my investigation with those in the author Walter Dickson's novels from the same industrial region.

In the book's preface I compared my experiences from the New England industrial town with those I obtained earlier from New England's agricultural region, particularly New Sweden, Maine, which I published in 1975. Throughout I dealt with characteristics, continuity, and the changes. The conditions for Swedes in respect to regions were considered according to location and social status. Likenesses and differences were illustrated in questions of religion, cultural evaluations, social life, disposition to organize, ethnic relations, and ethnic consciousness. The goal was to document the Swedes' and their descendants' histories of every-day life.

With comparisons between New Britain and the town of Pullman during the decade around the turn of the century, when Swedes constituted about six and ten percent, respectively, of the towns' populations, it is apparent that several contributions to the pattern stand out as similar for both of the small towns in the shadow of big cities.

In the study of New England I gave examples of how Swedish-owned firms advertised. On the following pages I tell how advertising was introduced in the Elim Church members' newspaper for the town of Pullman. Michigan Avenue in Roseland constituted the shopping thoroughfare, and here were the best Swedish shops, which served the employees and their families. As we see, A. Gustaf Bloom, tel. Pullman 6452, will "graciously recommend" all kinds of meat. E. Karlsson also speaks in English to other than Swedes; "very best repairing neatly done." Pearson and Malmström claims "All kinds of eyeglasses are made to order for whichever eye you prefer." At K. T. Thureson you find the lowest prices. Lundberg offers furniture and his services as a funeral director. Oscar Seagren promises quick and cheap painting, and "honest treatment." And Helen Ergo, owner of the New Swedish Bakery, promises to have cakes, pie, and all kinds of cookies "always at hand."

Such shopping establishments did not exist in the town of Pullman nor have I found any bookstores there. J. E. Hultgren in New Britain, "The town's oldest Swedish business" boasts, however, "dealing in Swedish books." The book lover in Pullman had only to go to the Pullman library, but it was not entirely gratis, and the books were chosen by Pullman himself or by his staff members. Notice the great difference! Freedom in the town of Pullman was never total.[1]

In New Britain the big industries were: North and Judd Company (1812), The Stanley Works (1835), Landers (1842), The Skinner Chuck Company (1887), New Britain Machine Company (1895), and Fafnir Bearing Company (1911). In the town's coat of arms is the inscription: "The hive around which the bees buzz and are busy." This applied to what was and is still the town's big industrial area. It is situated in the center of town as are the dwellings, but both began to move to the town's periphery after the Second World War.

Here also a similarity existed in that the dwellings in New Britain became mostly rented out to Puerto Ricans by the central renting agency; then the Swedes and other North Europeans moved out to the town's periphery; and in the town of Pullman the South Europeans and Hispanics likewise moved in; then the Swedes and other North Europeans moved out of the workers' housing.

The designs of homes and factories in New England's industrial towns had their prototypes in those of the English textile industries. As to the question of the recruitment of Swedish workers to the industries in New Britain I found that the most came from Jönköping, and the Älvsborg, and Halland counties. Inter-marriages seemed not to have been common, but when they occurred, the woman or man was of British origin.

In my quest to describe the condition of Swedes in New England's industrial towns, I obtained good help through the author Walter Dickson's impressionistic scenes in several of his books. In *America*, for example, where the story begins in the war year 1917, he has the protagonist Lars explain how it was when Swedish-Americans were caught in "the winds of progress" in the new land: "Here they dealt with their own strength. Here it was clear to them what they were good for. No royal Swedish jealousy that picks away at the youth who come with new understanding." But Lars had also seen contrasts; the miserable and the people who had been successful. Lars decided to write about this in the "big letter to his father." But it never amounted to more than a Christmas card and some boastful lines. This lack of enterprise was widespread enough but we also have invaluable evidence to the contrary.

In his *America* novel Walter Dickson discusses further the conditions in manufacturing and in construction; how living was shaped in different parts of the town, and how the different nationalities were treated. The books contain peoples' thoughts and feelings, a subject matter not easy to express except where in writers' pictures and metaphors they become poems and reality.

In *a glance* at the housing patterns it is known that young men often roomed with some family or in a boardinghouse. In the case of the married, the young pair were often tenants in apartments in the center of town, consisting of one to two rooms and kitchen in a stone apartment house of four to five flats, or in "three decker" homes built of wood and often by Swedish builders in New Britain, while those in the town of Pullman were mixed together in one of Pullman's three-flat brick houses. In other cases, in some apartment building in the immediate vicinity of the town of Pullman, or perhaps even in their own house in neighboring Roseland if finances would allow the investment in a house.

It happened that the Swedes' arrival at both areas was approximately simultaneous. Social thought was that the Swedes in New Britain had attained a better position with more who became doctors and builders than was the case in Pullman.

Where it applies to religious and cultural evaluations, or the social life and the character of organizations, the church held a strong position and cultivated the associations of company components and of different special interests. The Swedes in New Britain became well known through song and music, particularly in their famous Gunnar Wennerberg Choir. Compare the winning records of Swedes in some of Pullman's famous sports teams which I will take up in Chapter VII on Pullman characteristics.[2]

In some areas in New Britain Swedes were in a secure majority but in others there could be antagonisms such as fights with the Irish, and also with Yankees. The Swedes felt more sorry for the Polish, who often lived in poverty. They competed with the Italians in the work places, and they had several things in common with the Germans. However, their loyalty to them was put to the test during the World War. Earlier confrontations were brought under control in good cooperation. In this way the Swedish churches were opened to other nationalities. Because many of the Swedish descendants in New Britain moved out to the city's periphery, the ethnic institutions in the downtown area were weakened.

Living in New Britain meant shopping and amusing oneself in the big city, which was Hartford. In the town of Pullman it was naturally Chicago. For the inhabitants of New Britain traveling to Hartford it meant coming in to enjoy the big city's possibilities in all areas. But to take the streetcar from the town of Pullman to Chicago meant coming into a world-class city; from the production of railroad cars to recreation in the pubs; in cafes, hotels, theaters, and all they offered; to all the big office buildings and warehouses; and to specialists of different kinds. Chicago, which at one time was the USA's biggest city, was also number two among the world's Swedish cities, only surpassed by Stockholm.

Glimpses of the city

The Swedish immigrants' transplanting and the innovations of the Swedish heritage are described in a number of articles in *Swedish-American Life in Chicago. Cultural and Urban Aspects of an Immigrant People* 1850-1930, 1981. They reflect the variety in the world of Chicago Swedes; the variety of antagonisms, of different interests and organizations, churches, societies, and clubs. They also provide a good insight into life in Chicago.

Those for the Pullman residents were the festive occasions of going to the theater and seeing performances in Swedish and at the same time meeting their countrymen. Lars Furuland's essay, *From Värmländers to Slavs in Molokstorp-Swedish-American Theater in Chicago,* demonstrates it for us. F. A. Dahlgren, Frans Hodell, August Blanche, and Frans Hedberg were among the most appreciated playwrights. A popular drama was August Blanches' *Engelbrekt and His Dalkarlian* [a man from the province of Dalarna in Sweden], Zackarias Topelius' *Regina von Emmeritz* made a success when it had its premier at North Side Turner Hall in 1889. *The Värmlanders* played in the same theater in 1884. It was kept in the repertory from 1884 to 1950, along with those plays that deserve the name Swedish national drama in USA. According to Furuland, they really are Värmlander. It can be explained that the love between Erik and Anna transcended class boundaries; any who were conspicuous as immigrants, and those tragicomic plays containing song, dance, and music of a typical Swedish nature are, "an ideal cultural expression of Swedish America's attempt to save something of its identity as an ethnic group."

The cultural and political activities of Swedish-Americans and their relations to the receiving country inhabitants as well as other immigrant groups constitute a goal for the majority of all the researchers in the book. And, as August Palm expressed it in 1901, Chicago was "full of scoundrels and industrial barons. Chicago–the most American of all America's cities–a uniquely wonderful saga."

Per Nordahl also reminds us about it in his essay, *Swedish-American Labor in Chicago.* The city was the center of the Swedish labor movement, and Nordahl well knows the "Lake View Scandinavian Socialist Club" and the corporative and temperance supporting "Café Idrott." In such things the workers had experience from the labor movement's educational activities. Swedish radicals developed their own activities from this and at the same time formed a social network based upon ethnic fellowship.

H. Arnold Barton belonged to those who summarized the role America came to play for many Swedes: "For some a dream, for others a nightmare. For all, a vision of a modern world to come–for better or for worse," p. 110.

Harald Runblom, in his essay, *Chicago Compared: Swedes and Other Ethnic Groups in American Cities,* shows that when Swedes married outside their own group like Norwegians on the one hand and Danes on the other, they made up an extensive statistical compilation from the Federal Census, and reached ahead to come into more responsible positions. This applies more to Swedes in Rockford, Moline, Jamestown, and Worcester than to those in Chicago, P. 85.

Joy K. Lintleman, in his essays, *On my Own...,P. 97,* portrays the Swedish housekeepers' situation in Chicago; how they maintained rather good social status, and how they, above all, signified an emancipation for this group.

Anita R. Olson, in *The Community Created: Chicago Swedes 1880-1920,* has a map, p.52, showing Swedish areas, from Andersonville in the north to Pullman-Roseland in the south with parks and meeting places. The Westgöta Guild met in Viking Temple and Småland's Alliance met in Verdandi Hall–this is particularly noted with thoughts of my visits there.

Another insight into Chicago is presented in Gustaf Gullberg's *The book of Chicago–Sketches from a Trip to the Worlds Fair in 1893.* I turned over its pages from my actual sight angle, that is, how I thought that Swedes in the town of Pullman would view it and use it. Perhaps not so many Swedes were there, but probably enough so that the exhibits did not go by unnoticed.

Gustaf Gullberg gave his impressions in "sketches," as he called them. They are a festive portrayal of the business center from the Chicago River to Van Buren Street, of State Street with department stores, of South Water Street with farm products, Lake Street with stoneware shops, of Monroe Street with banks, Adams with the post office, Jackson with the Board of Trade and the unparalleled railroad stations, of Michigan Avenue with, as we already know, its offices and residences, and added to that, several big hotels. Dearborn Street with agencies, tailors, and book printers. LaSalle Street with steamship agents and insurance companies, and on Fifth Avenue [Wells St.] the newspaper street, and Franklin and Market Street with garment houses and shoe factories. Ship movements were greatest as far as 22nd Street, the animal and meat businesses were concentrated south of 39th St. with stockyards, slaughter houses, meat packing, and workers' housing–"a city within a city", p.79.

The north and south sides contained the prominent dwelling areas. The finest were south on Michigan Avenue, down South Park, along Lake Shore Drive and Lincoln Park and their surroundings.

At State Street, south of Polk Street, lived the city's black and yellow people along with Greeks. On the north side along Milwaukee Avenue lived Norwegians, Danes, Polish, and Germans. Chicago Avenue and the bordering streets could be called the Swedish streets, but overall in the district they also had Germans. The Swedish commissioner's office was located at 2342 Indiana Avenue. Along the north side were the Irish.

Gullgerg's portrayal of the fish market is colorful in his comparison of the American to the Swedish way of preparing fish, p. 82.

The fish market at Lake Street is the largest; yes, the largest in the entire West.

Here in large open shop windows the bounty of the sea's riches are displayed this way on the sidewalks and half way out on the street, large and small fishes, salt and fresh water fish, oysters, lobsters, crabs, clams, and snails, and live turtles. Ah! How a Swedish housewife's mouth would water if she had such a fish market to go to and shop. That would be something! But look! The good Americans do not understand the benefits of the rich seas they have at hand, for all these heavenly luscious fish are, meant for some specific American kitchen, soon to be declared inedible!

There are two heavenly streets for a gourmet to wander in, South Water Street and Lake Street!

Grapes and pears from California, oranges from Florida, bananas and pineapples from Cuba, peaches from Delaware, all kinds of berries from Michigan!

And then salmon from the Pacific Ocean, pike from Mexico Bay, lake sole from Lake Superior, Chicken, wild bear meat, frogs, rabbits, lovely food; you will find it all here in endless quantities, all streaming here from every part of the United States, and from these two streets these delights are then distributed to all cities!

The festivities are also found in the crowds on State Street, p.85.

Here, south of Marshall Field's the thickest crowds begin, the most colorful clutter on State Street, its center point is here.

Go there in the afternoon between two and five! There you will experience a sight that no other city can offer you! A mass of people undulating along the road-wide sidewalks and streaming in and out of shops, the street filled with streetcars and carriages, rolling in all directions, driving crosswise, whole trains of cable cars, ringing and jangling to warn the mass of people who, with the help of police, try to cross the street. What a cosmopolitan heap that tumbles from here!

The country's aborigines, the redskins, with black eyes, long hair, skin trousers, and cylinder hats! Yankees with hats back on their necks and hands in trouser pockets; Chinese with silk skull caps, dark blue cloaks, and black silk slippers; Negroes, wooly haired, ragged and shabby; and Negro ladies, colorful as Peter's painted cottage.

Rough Kentucky men, long-haired Californians, dark-complexioned southerners, nuns in black and white beside colorful creole dress, Turks in turbans, and Arabs in white mantles, Europeans of all kinds and all nationalities, dandys and ragamuffins, and among all these the screaming newsboys, the stubborn bootblacks, hurry through like snakes within the crowd.

You hear all the world's languages spoken–it is like being at Babel!

The corner of State and Madison is where the crowd is at its high point. This corner of the city is where the greatest number of people pass daily.

Here are found the largest ladies shops and fashionable women in Chicago stop to meet here for an "after shopping" meeting at Chicago's fashionable café, the colorfully decorated, glittering "Gunthers".

And when evening falls, the life of the district takes on an even more fantastic appearance. Then the skyscrapers are lit from top to bottom with thousands of electric lights blazing in all colors; but don't be satisfied with white or yellow lights; all the colors in the world are used. The walls and ceilings in many of the largest shops on the ground floors are often done completely on all sides in faceted mirrors which shine their hundred lights in a thousand light clusters, enticing people and coloring the street for a long way like light-blazing butterflies.

Marshall Field's was a department store that employed 3000 people. As a matter of preference they "loved to employ Swedes." They had many living nearby; also on Clark Street, where I worked one time at the Swedish American Museum, but in Gullberg's time he seemed to find more Jews, Greeks, Italians, Chinese and Blacks. North of Van Buren one put himself up in the "better parts" at the Grand Pacific Hotel, which competed with the Palmer House in luxury.

The Columbian Exposition

The sight of the Columbian Exposition came first from a pleasure boat starting at Van Buren via Jackson Park and the Columbian Pier. The experiences began at the Women's Exhibition Building, the Gardening Exhibits Building, the Japanese Phoenix Palace, the Transportation Building with a complete railroad train, buildings for mining, and for electricity with a kino-photograph room which prepared snapshots, The Industrial Palace is the largest building "which the hand of man has ever erected, 30 ½ acres of floor space and room for 300,000 people." In the building for agriculture and forestry, products from the whole world are shown. Nearby stands the fish exhibits building with the aquarium, and everything in it fades by comparison with Norway's impressive collection of fishing gear and fish products. If one feels hungry there is the Swedish restaurant with a good dinner for a reasonable price.

During his visit to the Columbian Exposition, "the greatest show on earth," Gullberg gave directions to hotels, tours by buggy and cabs, cable cars, horse-drawn streetcars, and elevated railroads. The exposition would have you be seen in electric boats, or up high in electric trains, or in Indian sedan chairs. The Swedish Pavilion lay diagonally across from the fisheries exhibition in the northeast area of the grounds. Skånska Cement had constructed two stories and in the rooms one could study fine collections from Bofors, Ankarsrum, Domnarvet, Avesta, Uddeholm, Rörstrand, Huskvarna, Slöjdföreningen, Nordiska Museum, and Munksjö. Hellberg's punch from Götgatan was not forgotten. In the Swedish Arts Exhibition hung pictures by Zorn, Liljefors, Nordström, Kreuger, Carl Larsson, and there stood sculptures by Christian Ericson, Hasselberg, and Nyström. Gullberg closed his round of exhibitions by declaring that Sweden will no doubt be keenly observed and accepted seriously out here in spite of its smallness, its poverty, and its "remoteness."

"City of the Century"

The Columbian Exposition was arranged, of course, to celebrate the 400-year anniversary of Columbus' landing in the West Indies. And because of this Chicago suddenly introduced itself to the whole world as the American center of modernity with a newly-built city. "The White City designed by Burnham" also had a central place in a newly-published book "City of the Century" by Donald L. Miller, 1996.

A prominent place here also goes to G. M. Pullman in the chapter, "The Pullman Idea." In a review of Miller's book written by Sven Widmalm under the headline "Chicago steps out of the ashes and reaches for the sky" in *Svenska Dagbladet* 10-13-96, Widmalm takes particular notice of Chicago's elevation by several meters from the swamp level. In this, Pullman was one of the leaders. In his youth he had specialized in the raising of houses and his workers dug down under the buildings' foundations where they placed timbers. Then they were lifted with the help of jacks at the same time that a new foundation was quickly built. To lift the Tremont House required 1,200 men operating 5,000 jacks, and this was all performed while normal activity continued in the building. It was after continuing in the house lifting business that Pullman created his own industry. In 1865 he began to build wider and bigger railroad cars equipped with walnut paneling and plush upholstering. Then followed, as we know, in the beginning of the 1880 decade, the establishment of the factories and the town of Pullman. There bordellos and political organizations were barred, and labor unions also were forbidden. Pullman also exerted control over the only newspaper, *The Pullman Journal*. But after the strike in 1894 the myth of the good industrial patriarch was smashed, and after his death his body was laid in a lead-sealed casket in concrete to prevent vandalizing the remains.[3]

Sven Widmalm places Pullman among the greatest of the industrialists and business men who led the expansion of Chicago. Others were Marshall Field, the department store king, Aaron Montgomery Ward and Richard Warren Sears, mail order sales pioneers, Philip Danforth Armour, the man who created the worlds largest meat packing industry, Charles Tyson Yerkes, streetcar magnate who succeeded in forcing upon the city a rational communications system. It was in the same colorful way that Pullman asserted himself. In his review, Widmalm regarded Donald L. Miller as sometimes too hasty in accepting Chicagoans' image of themselves, but considers him a skillful historian. To those who wish to broaden their perspectives he recommends reading William Cronon's "Nature's Metropolis", 1991. Cronon points out actually, the simultaneous and mutually related development of cities, of communications, and the exploitation of nature. According to his analysis Chicago was formed by the historic cooperative powers where private individuals were more or less capable of mastering the growth of a new type of big city and a new type of ecology. Cronon presents a historical insight, while Miller deals with an epoch, "but he did that skillfully."

> Donald L. Miller's chapter headings also furnished the basis for legends. I am thinking of such as "City of Dreamers and Doers," "The Mechanical Man," "Emporia, City of the West," "My Lost City," "Lets Build Ourselves a City," "The Pullman Idea," "Stories in Stone and Steel," "Burnham's White City," "The New Chicago Woman," and "If Christ Came to Chicago."

Miller, in this second principal work, the eighteenth chapter (II: 8 B, p. 228) titled, "The Pullman Idea," regards Pullman as probably the most famous American when the great exposition was opened: "When the Columbian Exposition opened, George Pullman was probably the best known Chicago name throughout America, as well as abroad." The statement is supported by a lengthy article in *The London Times* about the remarkable railroad titan and city-builder: "...and when prominent visitors came to Chicago he liked to take them out to it [the exposition] in his special rail car, a sixty seven foot-long mansion on wheels with its own servants' quarters." *The Times* summarized:

> The story of Pullman naturally divides itself into three parts, the building of the car, the building of the operating system, and the building of the town. From gossip sources we are also certain that Pullman was a strict pedant, a regular martinet. The beloved child was Florence, and he named his town's hotel in her honor. Otherwise he had rather few friends but played poker now and then at his club. He enjoyed visiting his mother's apartment in New York and during his scarcely existent leisure time he resided either alone at Castle Rest on the St. Lawrence river or with his wife Harriet at Elberon, near Long Branch, New Jersey, which he built in the 1870s. During the exposition year his architects, S. Spencer Beman and Nathan F. Barret made good revenue for their contributions to the appearance of the factories, row houses, and parks. At the same time they contributed designs at Washington Park and the Grand Central railroad terminal.

Donald L. Miller's particular chapter about the exposition is called "1893" and it is preceded by "The New Chicago" and "Burnham's White City." Among the industrialists the architects stand out as the chief figures in his story: The skyscraper architecture pioneers, Daniel Burnham, John Wellborn Root, and Louis Sullivan. The latter was, of course, the mentor of Frank Lloyd Wright.

Burnham, the White City's chief architect, also placed his impression on the well-known Museum of Science and Industry, Art Institute, and Public Library, all in the European Classicism. The pioneer work in 1890-1900 foretold the modern functionalism. Fredrik Law Olmsted, the creator of the parks in Chicago, New York, and New Britain, also belonged to this famous school. The Chicago suburb, Riverside is included here also. The Olmsted traditions consist of quality with variety, rhythm, and not the least, stress on the contribution of landscaping.

Pullman had shown the way as a rational organizer and builder of cities. In "The North American Industrial Community" in *Historic Buildings Magazine*, 1987, p.33, Mats Ahnlund and Lasse Brunnström summarized their views of American planning traditions as the sources of inspiration for 20th Century industrial architecture, and Elias Cornell observed that people in America understood that the shaping of the whole was most important among planning problems, and calls Fredrik Law Olmsted the shaper of the combined objectives of city building and park architecture.

> The White City's classical style is perceived as a justified expression, which Elias Cornell, however, questioned. " How could this be"? He asks in *The History of Great Exposition Architecture,* 1952, p. 183, and answers that, "Innovation in the shaping of a national enterprise is probably of the most importance. The classical education of architects came to the rescue in a situation that seemed not at all clear. Through the application of classical architecture to the largest exposition the world had seen, the Americans obviously wanted to demonstrate to themselves and others that they in the end had the same involvement in the classic heritage as all other nations."

In conclusion, it is interesting to observe that the architects' participation in the town of Pullman, in the White City, and in Chicago, was especially meaningful. Unfortunately, on July 5, 1894, the gleaming white city was destroyed in a fire, which was the worst to happen in Chicago since 1871.[4] The depression and the strike of 1894, and the subsequent train of events contributed to the death of the industrial patriarch, G.M. Pullman in 1897, and thereby the regression of the town of Pullman.

The paternalism of the 1800s had weakened the town of Pullman's key role as model communities began to play out their role. This was also the fate of Carnegie's Klippan in Göteborg. But both would be rehabilitated thanks to their great architectural and socio-historical value and be declared cultural treasures, both in the shadow of a large city; the town of Pullman in the shadow of one of the world's very largest cities. Thus the attractive neighborhoods again became good investments for the future.

---

[1] At this time public libraries in Illinois charged fees ranging up to eight dollars per year. The first free libraries endowed by the industrialist Andrew Carnegie began to appear in 1889.
Raymond Bial and Linda LaPuma Bial The Carnegie Library in Illinois (Urbana and Chicago: University of Illinois Press) [no date]
Mr. Pullman, during his lifetime, firmly believing that everything worth having in life is better appreciated if a sacrifice, however small, be made for the desired object, established a library membership fee of $3.00 per year for adults and $1.00 per year for those under eighteen years of age, with the express understanding that all money collected in this way should go towards the purchase of new books, The Pullman Company paying all the running expenses. This arrangement continued until 1908, when the Pullman Public Library became the Pullman Public Free Library.
Bertha Stewart Ludlam, "Pullman Library Full of Local Romance," *The Calumet Index,* (October 12, 1917)

[2] The Pullman Band was equally famous, enjoying a national reputation. Starting in June, 1886, the Pullman Band gave a series of free concerts in Arcade Park. The company had erected a large bandstand and thousands of people regularly attended the concerts. On November 8, 1895, the Pullman Band numbering eighty pieces left Chicago for a trip through the South.
J. F. Hostrawser "Reminiscences of the Pullman Band," The Pullman Car Works Standard, (Vol II Number 9, January, 1918)

[3] It was common practice during this era for the wealthy to take similar measures for burial to avoid being victimized by grave robbers who sought jewelry for its resale value. However, Liston Leyendecker says, "For some time prior to his death, Pullman had worried that his corpse might be kidnaped by disgruntled former employees; to prevent possible desecration, he had his grave prepared accordingly." Liston Edgington Leyendecker, Palace Car Prince (Niwot, CO: University Press of Colorado, 1992), p. 258

[4] Fire destroyed some of the buildings in the exposition while it was being razed after its closing in 1893. Suggestions had been made for preserving the White City, but on January 8, 1894, incendiaries burned the Casino, Peristyle, and Musical Hall. Then on the evening of July 5, 1894, the Terminal Station caught fire. *The Chicago Herald* reported on July 6 that casualties included the Administration, Mining, Manufactures, Agriculture, and Electricity Buildings.

From Our Community, Vol. 1, no. 3, pages 8 and 9.

*Advertisements for the nearby shops on Michigan Ave., Roseland.
From* The Luther Banner, *1912. A publication of Elim Lutheran Church.*

Chapter VII
Their Employer
The Strike!

"Conflicts between management and employees were eased in conferences, but on the owners' terms," write Mats Ahnlund and Lasse Brunnström regarding New England's early industrial communities in their study from 1987, P. 32. The Pullman establishment was based on a completely regulated and paternalistic company and town. This model implies, of course, that in principle, Pullman's family and company owned all and regulated all in the closed community. The entire surroundings reminded the workers of the factory and their work in them even after the work day ended.

Characteristic of the 12% Swedish contribution to the population in the town of Pullman (but earlier nearly 20% were employed at this workplace) was a general satisfaction with the long two-story row houses and the double houses, the landscaping, and the sports structures. They did not have the equivalent in Sweden.

The Pullman News

The company publication, *The Pullman News*, which served as the local newspaper, also reflected the company owners' viewpoints, and in my review of the annual issues that were available at my visit to The Newberry Library Archives in Chicago, I found no critical comment against the company, at least in the archives that I went through.

The company paper seemed to mix news from the business with notices about different personnel groups and about particular persons. Particular attention was given to employees who performed their work in a commendable manner. New pensioners and those with service anniversaries were also recognized in the family pages. Conductors and Porters held a prominent place among these. Leisure time interests were given space in its columns, especially reports from the sports arenas.

Samples from the paper include such features as: praise for the company's accomplishments; for individuals; jests and seriousness; "pests," "glossaries," "jingles"; verses about "The Pullman Man"; and much more.

John Fridell, "Old Reliable John" was born 12/22/1866 at the village of Lidköping, Sweden. Mr. Fridell came to Pullman in 1892 and was employed as an axle turner in which trade he was an expert. *Pullman News*, 1922, p. 81.

In 1922 (page 174), a dinner was given at the Calumet Commercial Club for Charles August Jonson, who had started at Pullman in 1882. In 1923, (page 7), the following were awarded: Carpenter Carl A. Carlson, 66, employed in January 1880, general worker Gustaf Person, 63, employed in June 1880, "trans. cond." August Andersson, 64, employed in April, 1881, finish carpenter Anton B. Anderson, 64, employed in May, 1881, Inspector Iwan Tornquist, 65, employed in June, 1881, Group Chief, Claus W. Wenstrom, 60, employed in June, 1882, Repairman Henoch Anderson, 65, employed in July 1882, and Gate Watchman Gustaf F. Hedin, employed in September 1881.

Particular attention was given to baseball and cricket where the different districts and factories took part in the industrial leagues. Periodically the Pullman teams were also in the national series. Success and adversity were also reported in the local newspapers. *The South End Reporter,* a paper for the communities of Pullman and Roseland on the south side of Chicago, had for many years a sports journalist named Racine Thompson. On October 23, 1968 the paper printed a whole section about his activities through the years: "He is still going strong at 79. He has written articles for the Reporter for over 60 years." The headline reads, "Racine tells it like it was way back then." He was born in Norway, came to Pullman in 1905, where he worked in the Clock Tower Building. He was married to a Swede, Anna Peterson, whom he had met at a gymnastic function at Turner Hall.

In the article are results, episodes, players, anecdotes, and much more. The pictures show teams and team rosters. Here I present two of them; the Pullman teams from 1892 and 1913.

In the "Pullman Boys Baseball Club" there were two Swedes in 1892, Oscar Dahlin and Henry Aurelius. On the Marlowes Football Team of 1907, one, Arvid Lund. On the TornadoFootball Team, one, A. Weberg. On the Pullman Company Baseball Team of 1908, one, Charles Lundahl, and on the Palmer Park Track Team of 1912, one, B. Peterson. The "Pullman Cricket Team" won the Cricket Championship in 1913, and their soccer team was known to be the best in all America at one time. They won "The City Championship" several times and also the so-called "Peter Peel Championship."

Some other rather well-known Swedes were S. J. Hagman, born 1897 in Uppsala, Thore Sundberg, born 1894 in Tidaholm, and Jim Wolff, born 1898 in Lysekil. They played on the football team "Swedish Americans" in Chicago. Famous was Herbert "The Wall" Carlson, defected international team player from IFK Göteborg, who began an American professional boxing career in The Viking Corporation, 1922; Sven Nordin, born in Sandviken in 1899 and boxed in the Sture Athletic Club, Chicago, 1923; Ernest Viberg, manager for Viking Corp. from 1921, who served as sports trainer at Columbia University. Gunnar Persson tells more of the last named category in his book, *The First Professional Boxers,* 1996.

Racine Thompson's memoir also covers ice skating on Lake Calumet, gymnastic exhibitions, jumping contests, and sprint running in Palmer Park and at other sports arenas. Swedes who took part here were Gillie Billstrand, Charlie Brandt, Hjalmar Erickson, Axel Lindskog, H. Swanson, and Harry Tornquist. In addition, Brandt and Tornquist were outstanding football players with the "Thistles" and the "Eclipse" respectively.

An early map from 1885 shows the short distance between Pullman, the open air regions, sports arenas, and Lake Calumet. The opportunities to participate in sports were therefore good for youth who grew up in the Pullman-Roseland region.

I began this chapter with an analysis of the conflict between management and employees, and will continue the subject here.

We have established that the company newspaper was one-sided in presenting the factory leadership's policies, the continuing progress of the company in the different districts and within departments, how management called attention to the employees' achievements: praise received by the conductors, faithfulness to the employees who lived their lives in the service of the company, songs and verses about the idealized company, sports presentations by the Pullman teams, etc.

Here, I had only one side but on one occasion I found some "objections," some critical questions from the employees aimed at the factory management, and not in the company paper's own columns either.

The consequences of the company's paternalistic attitudes towards the model community were not wholly negative. The positive ones were the strong motive forces that led to the company's progress, and the engaging aspects of the architecture and planning, those which were developed into the model community.

On the other hand, the over-patronizing and controlling policies were enforced from the management side, leading gradually to the collective reactions from the employees; those which contributed to the crushing, devastating strike.

This, of course, had not in the least been the purpose intended by the company newspaper as it reflected the changes.

A question that I asked in this connection is how order was maintained. They don't mention the police, but it is possible that over and above the controlling policies, hired detectives and strike breakers were used.

The strike "The Time's snake would shed its skin"

This great conflict culminated in the infamous Pullman Strike, which is mentioned in a different connection in one of my other chapters, but which obviously must now have its place here.

Almont Lindsey has published a close study of the Pullman strike in his 1942 thesis, *The Pullman Strike*, 385 pages, Illustrated. The basic material is drawn from archives that he found in the Pullman collection in the John Crerar Library; Pullman Branch Library; the State Archives, Springfield; and the Library of Congress.

He had also gone through newspapers from the actual period, like the Chicago Chronicle, Chicago Daily News, Chicago Herald, Chicago Times, Chicago Tribune, and Harper's Weekly. Also literature like Grover Cleveland's *The Government in the Chicago Strike of 1894*; McAlister Coleman's *Eugene V. Debs*, 1930; Henry J. Ford's *The Cleveland Era*, 1919; James Henry's *Richard Olney and His Public Service*, 1923; Allan Nevin's *Letters of Grover Cleveland*, 1933; *United States Strike Commission Report*, 1895; Horace White's *The Life of Lyman Trumbull*, 1913; and George M. Pullman's own *The Strike of Pullman*, 1894.

Among chapter titles are: Growth of the Model Town, Paternalism, Origin of the Pullman Strike, The American Railway Union at the General Managers' Association, The Storm Breaks, Federal Intervention, The Policy of Illinois Officials, Progress of the Strike in Chicago, Nation-Wide Character of the Struggle, and Public Opinion and the Press.

Among the illustrations are: The principle character, George M. Pullman; Eugene V. Debs, trade union leader; Governor John P. Altgeld; Pullman's Administration Building; Hotel Florence; The Arcade and Lake Vista. The burning of seven hundred freight cars on the Panhandle railroad south of Fiftieth Street, Chicago, July 6, 1894; and national guardsmen firing into the mob at Loomis and Forty-ninth Street, Chicago, July 7, 1894, are reproduced here.

It is common knowledge, supported by Almont Lindsey's untangled detail, that the Pullman strike of 1894 threatened a whole nation with social and economic upheaval. Of course, the strike was not only a local conflict but culminated in an explosion in the relationship between labor and capital. Woven into his report are the ups and downs of the whole remarkable "Pullman experiment"; as Lindsey sees it, a unique kind of philanthropic project conceived by an employer for his employees. But the "Baronet" began to rule with a too-strong iron hand. Here it can also be attested that Swedes had been involved in the strike.

Of particular interest are the reactions of the press in the wake of the strike. On the editorial pages of the Chicago Herald and the Chicago Tribune they expressed no great sympathy for the workers' organization, but on the news pages described the events with an undertone of understanding and sympathy for the workers. The "American Railway Union" also went directly in "medias res" and directed a demand to the city officials to stop advertising in these papers.

The union's executive leadership, "the headquarters" claimed that the press did not provide the public with information about the situation, and urged people to express sympathy for the workers by wearing a white ribbon on their coat sleeves until the fight was over. To their joy the next day produced "an epidemic of white ribbon," which was worn not only by the workers but by a large number of sympathizers among the public.

The Chicago Dispatch, the Chicago Mail, and the Chicago Times took up the strikers' cause but the size of their circulation could not be compared with those of the biggest papers who stood on the employer's side.

Some papers drew a distinction, however, between the different striking parties; the American Railway Union, and the local strike comprised of the Pullman employees. Still others sharply condemned G. M. Pullman's labor policies. The Chicago Herald in an editorial of July 4th aimed just as much criticism at the American Railway Union as they did at Pullman. The paper took up the treatment that Pullman's employees were exposed to. This should not be forgotten, even if the position of these workers came to be placed in the background of the gigantic fight which began to blow up the whole country. And there was no mistaking the fact that the papers felt compassion for the hungry and underpaid workers at Pullman.

The Chicago Tribune pointed out in an editorial that even if the labor leaders' actions were unacceptable, that did not free Pullman from the responsibility to work for a peaceful solution.

No editorials were more contemptuous towards Pullman, however, than those in the Chicago Times, wherein he was characterized as a Richard III and provided with a spiteful countenance.

The only newspaper that stood completely on Pullman's side during the strike was the New York World. Their opinion was that if Pullman chose to stand firm, the arbitrators would probably understand his case. Only think, said the paper, of all the owners whose businesses are destroyed, who are strangled, and most of all the sacrifice of human life. Lindsey, p. 317-318.

The events of the strike are summarized in the Encyclopedia Britannica, 1933, p. 797, with these lines:

> On June 26, Eugene V. Debs and the American Railway Union launched a sympathetic boycott of all Pullman's cars. When the railroads retaliated by firing union members, the union struck the railroads, and by the end of the month the work stoppage had spread across the country.

> On June 30, U. S. Attorney General Richard Olney deputized 3600 men to keep the trains running, and on July 2, he obtained a federal court injunction prohibiting interference with the trains. When a rioting mob wrecked a mail train the next day, President Cleveland ordered troops into Chicago. By July 20 the troops had been withdrawn but the trains were running under military guard. Government intervention had spelled defeat for the union. In 1895, the U. S. Supreme Court upheld the government's use of an injunction in a labor dispute, providing the enemies of labor with a potent weapon.

> The town of Pullman was annexed by the City of Chicago in 1889. Therefore the city took over the maintenance of streets, fire and police protection, and other functions. In 1927 Pullman Incorporated was formed, with the Pullman Company and the Pullman Car & Manufacturing Co. as its principal subsidiaries. In 1930 it was enlarged by the purchase of several car works. Through the federal decision of 1944, however, the company was ordered by the authority of the Sherman Act to decide either on car manufacturing or the leasing of Pullman cars to the railroad companies. The result was that Pullman retained the manufacturing but sold the service operations to a consortium consisting of 56 railroad companies. The car factories had a production capacity of about 100,000 cars per year.

Pullman Porters—painful reality

One group of employees has been an object of fine scrutiny. This has been done by Arthur C. McWatt, B. A. in social studies and M. A. in history from the University of Minnesota. The scrutinies apply to Pullman porters—personnel who followed the cars which were hired out to the different railroad companies. They constituted perhaps the best known of personnel categories at Pullman. His article was published in *Minnesota History*, Spring 1997, and was called "A Greater Victory. The Brotherhood of Sleeping Car Porters in St. Paul." The introduction to the article says:

> None can deny the genius of George Mortimer Pullman, whose palatial railroad cars created American luxury travel in the late nineteenth century. The flawless service that passengers came to expect on the Pullman cars depended on porters, African-American men who labored long hours under grueling conditions. Just as George Pullman retained ownership of all his rolling stock by leasing cars to railroads, he also maintained control over his workers—hiring, firing, and setting conditions of employment, 'Being on the road.'

This category of employee, of course, represented Pullman's public face to a high degree. The company demanded that they should be neatly dressed and always on the spot, always ready. Therefore they were also very much appreciated by the travelers.

Each of them was responsible for his car—receive passengers and their baggage, keep house in the car from day till night, prepare beds and draperies for the night, and then in the morning restore everything again; in between to perform innumerable small duties, and to always be at hand. Besides that, to brush all shoes that were placed in the corridors. The time taken for their own rest and sleep was minimal. When the travelers called them they used the sobriquet "George," completely a remnant from slavery times.

Their fight to get better working conditions went on continuously. They were expected to work about 400 hours per month at a low wage and that was completely contingent on tip money. Their position among the various personnel categories was low. It was therefore typical when Debs, in his role as "President of the radical American Railway Union" (ARU), during his work to organize personnel categories at Pullman in the 1890s, completely ignored them.

The American Federation of Labor (AFL) made attempts to organize them in 1909, 1910, and 1913. When, for example, Frank L. Boyd as chief negotiator of the AFL in 1912 made a proposal to raise their monthly wage from 25 dollars to 60, "working conditions did not improve and Boyd was branded a troublemaker." Instead of going to the arbitration table the company in 1912 formed "The Pullman Porters' Benefit Association," which hardly contained even a hope of destroying the professional organization.

This continued until 1925 before it got better. It was then they at last organized themselves more powerfully into "The Brotherhood of Sleeping Car Porters" (BSCP). Their opposition party, "The Pullman Palace Car Co." had already been established in 1866. BSCP chose Philip Randolph as chairman. He was born in Crescent City Florida, had worked as a porter and a "railroad waiter," before he became active in the labor movement and started the newspaper *The Messenger*. As the result of his ability he was called "the most dangerous Negro in America." In *The Messenger* he published the demand that the BSCP's members should have 150 dollars a month, tips should be abolished, the work hours should be shortened to 240 hours per month, being called "George" should disappear, and a guarantee should be given: part 1, four hours continuous nighttime sleep, part 2, the guarantee of receiving a pension of 16 dollars a month after 40 years service.

During the depression years around 1930 the arbitrations were put aside, but on June 27, 1935 a jubilant Philip Randolph could telegraph: "First victory of Negro workers over a great industrial corporation." The contract itself was signed by Pullman Company and by BSCP on August 25, 1937. It meant 175 dollars a month and 240 hours work per month.

But the negotiations, compromises, and attempts at mediation continued through the year, then to the federal level. The possibilities of advancement from Porter to "Conductor" were first opened in July, 1967. George Young from St. Paul MN became the first and he went to the Northern Pacific Railroad.

The decline of the railroads naturally diminished the numbers of Pullman Porters, but now even their turn came to be honored. President Franklin D. Roosevelt's Executive Order 8802 came as a general prohibition of racial discrimination, and in 1942 Philip Randolph was given the "Leaders' Medal" for his pioneering achievements. In 1964 he also received the Medal of Freedom–"the highest honor that can be given to civilians."

I have had a glimpse of how it has subsequently gone for this work category thanks to Raymond E. Johnson, who sent me a *Chicago Tribune* feature of February 14, 1997, and therefore I will close the chapter with a quote from the text. It reads:

> Two of the few surviving black Pullman attendants recount the bittersweet experience of working on the railroad before the civil rights movement on a whistlestop tour from Oakland CA to Chicago IL.

Two third-generation Pullman Porters, Virgil and Garrard Smock Jr., were invited to make a trip from Oakland to Chicago by Amtrak and to attend a banquet in the town of Pullman where at one time the sleeping cars were built. (Amtrak took over the intercity railroad passenger business in the year 1971.) At one of the large stations where the train made a stop, Bloomington-Normal, Illinois, Virgil Smock held a conversation and gave glimpses of his and his father's working lives. It was the usual thing that during their attendance they constantly spoke such phrases as, "Yes sir, your drinks coming right up, sir"! He thinks the present days are the greatest in his life. "Here I am, sitting down on a train with no work to do, enjoying the scenery of this beautiful country. And somebody else is bringing me the drinks."

Smock's grandfather was in the service of the Pullman Company for 27 years, and he died of a heart attack in 1929, just as he was busy making up a bed for the night. An uncle worked there from 1915 until 1950, and he himself had done so between 1930 and 1960, before Amtrak took over. Some passengers he had were Frank Sinatra, Joan Crawford, and Earl Warren. In St. Louis 91-year-old Felix Anderson came aboard this train, and he proudly confirmed that he had indeed served Harry Truman.

Together they also recalled when they could not come into the head office but "had to stand outside until a supervisor came out to give them orders."

But at a later time the porters have been able to see their sons and daughters go to college "and become doctors and lawyers who could perform their professions" said the men with emphasis at the end of the interview. From the *Chicago Tribune*, February 17, 1997.

And here I allow this chapter about several *characteristics,* some *patterns* at Pullman to end. Joy and grief alternated, conflicts arose and were resolved. Some categories stood in the limelight, others remained fairly obscure.

And we are certainly reminded of the special culture and unity which grew among the railroad men, especially strong in America with its enormous distances. And in closing, just their words, the group's own language. Some of them are expressions reproduced from the personnel publications and need no clarification, while others are special, such as, "make down" instead of "make up" the beds. Some are wonderfully colorful like, "candy run," "battleship," "bird cage," "brass hat," "riding the Indian blanket," and "my dogs bark."

The Pullman Boys Baseball Team, May, 1892, the 16-year-old champions of Chicago. From the back row, Albert Orne CF, Harry Ball SS, George McQueen 3B, Oscar Dahlin LF, Clarence Hatch 2B, Ed Action 1B, Capt. Tom Cooke RF, Horace Ball C, Harry Aurelius Mascot, and George Kunst. From The South End Reporter, *10/23/1968.*

Pullman's championship cricket team, 1913. From bottom left: H. Crowther, A. Van Deutekom, Wm. Balster, Rev. T. Hughes, B. Aston, President W. Scowcroft, E. H. Dixon, Ed Butcher, B. Govier, F. Wild, F. Philpott, J. P. Flinn, V. J. Smale, M. Turner Jr., Scorer C. Gordon, J. Philpott, Wm. Cummings, Vice President R. H. Adams. Photo The South End Reporter, *10/23/1968 in an article written by Racine Thompson.*

Eugene V. Debs. From Lindsey, The Pullman Strike, *1964, p. 110*

Chapter VIII
Their Job—
Coaches and Trains

In the magazine, *The Carbuilder,* we can follow Pullman Standard's manufactured product not only in Chicago but also in several branch plants all over the USA all the way to the year 1969; products such as the new steel cars in 1910, "The Virginia Dare" in 1927, streamlined trains in 1934, aluminum cars in 1942, "The 2639" in 1947, "The Cedar Rapids" and the "Skytop Cars" in 1948, "The Silver Terrace" and "The Superdome" in 1952. It can also be said that the Orient Express, which ran between 1883 and 1977 had dark blue Pullman cars and that the Orient Express was re-inaugurated in its new form in 1982.

George Mortimer Pullman had founded the "Pullman Palace Car Company" after his success with his first sleeping car. With money from a building enterprise in Chicago, he began his career there. With his assistant, Col. James H. Bowen, and with the sturdy help of several groups of carpenters and smiths, carpet layers and upholsterers under the guidance of Benjamin C. Field, he made the enterprise an enormous success. Production of "The Pioneer" started in 1864. In 1868 came the debut of "The Delmonico."

Improved sleeping car types were put on the longest stretches of track. In 1887 the bellows coupling was constructed, followed by the bogie construction, which stabilized the cars' under-carriage.

Dimensions of greater width

Newspaper articles from America had often described with admiration these Pullman innovations that had spread all over the world. Take for example V.G.S. Topsöe in the book, *From America,* printed in 1874 by Albert Bonnier, book printer. The 500-mile railroad trip between Chicago and Omaha he thought was a pleasure to make. Pullman made people forget they were riding a train, p.257. The twelve-wheeled cars made it pleasant. Silk sofas stood along the sides and between the sofas hung mirrors. The lounges and salons were converted to sleeping compartments. Even the knobs were polished. The carpenters had made panels of walnut and the wash stands had marble tops.

Many of these carpenters had come from Sweden. It is really about these and above all, a group among them, around whom my book revolves. Later in this chapter I will return to Nykyrke and Mullsjö and see how it fared with some of those in the third and fourth generation, but first a section comparing Pullman's technical achievements with others in the industry, followed by a part characterized by the concept, "Alle Züge nach Chicago."[1]

Great Britain probably built most of its cars in its own factories. In 1870, an American, W. D. Mann, founded a factory for "Boudoir Cars" in England. Pullman's idea of owning and operating sleeping cars was adopted in advance of all others in Europe by the Belgian engineer, Georges Nagelmackers, who in 1872, founded the international sleeping car company, Compagnie Internationale des Wagons-Lits. For several years in the beginning he had Mann as his partner, but they split up and in 1875 he reorganized the Wagons-Lit company in its final form. The company obviously did not build any cars but ordered them from different purveyors.

Already in the 1870s Pullman was attempting to bind the European buyers to him; especially those who had started such enterprises as the Midland Railway in England in 1874, where the cars were of the American type. Completely showing to his advantage, Pullman's cars were of broader width and greater weight.

In George Behrends book, *Pullman in Europe,* 1962, we find the motif of "Pullmans today and tomorrow," and in the 19th chapter we see names such as, *Bristol Pullman, Golden Arrow, Normandy Express, North Star, Simplon Orient Express, Southern Belle, South Wales Pullman, Western Riding Pullman,* and *Yorkshire Pullman.*

The Golden Arrow departed from platform 2, Victoria Station to Dover, page 129ff. Its cars were designed by Waring-Gilow and built at Preston Park Works. They were painted brown and white (the sleeping cars in blue), two 2nd class and seven 1st class cars included the Pegasus Trianon Bar, and a dining car and observation car. From Calais the train was called, *Fleche d'Or.* In Paris the train departed from the Gare du Nord and, for a time, from the Gare de Lyon.

The menus consisted of "chilled fruit juices, soup of the day, Omelets, lamb chop, Dover sole, minute steak, potatoes, vegetable, fruits of the season, quarter bottle of champagne, (the Pullman Company quarter bottles) and much more."

Of course in Sweden also, we were inspired to work up from a comfortable sleeping place in first class, to corridors in the car, to gas lighting, to vacuum brakes, and to a specially built restaurant car. Improvements in standards were introduced, first on the main lines, with the yearly report on the experiments accomplished.

Hans Lindblad and Ingvar Henricson have in their book *Round Trip to America,* 1955, p.193ff., taken a series of examples of how Swedish engineers came home with experiences from the USA, and what that meant in starting new impulses for Swedish technology and Swedish industry. With American experience as a foundation, Hugo Hammar, for example, built up the Göta Works into Sweden's leading shipyard. With him and a succession of young Swedish engineers, John Ericsson stood foremost as a favorite. Through the use of American production methods Sigfrid Edström took ASEA in Västerås, which found itself in crisis, and with swift diligence built it up into a major industry. They give many more examples of the influence from the USA, not the least, the Worlds Fair exhibit at Philadelphia in 1876, Chicago in 1893, and the fact that even the countless individual initiatives, by letter and other contacts, produced a great impetus for innovation.

When we consider some of the names of inventors and builders within the category of railroads during the 19th Century, aside from the name of G. M. Pullman, these are the ones who stand out as leaders:

John Haswell, Scotland: design of the locomotive, "Windobona," 1812.

Christopher Blackett, England: design of the locomotive, "Puffy Billy," 1813.

John Stevens, USA: design of the cog rail engine, 1825.

George Stephenson, England: design of the locomotive, "Witch," 1828 and "Planet," 1830.

Mare Sequin, France: design of the tube boiler, 1829.

Isaac Dripps, USA (Camden): improvement of "Planet," 1831.

James Brooks and Henry Campell [sic], USA (Philadelphia): design of the 8-wheeled bogie locomotive, 1836.

E. Walschaert, Belgium: design of the slide guide, 1844.

Heusiger von Waldegg: improvement of the locomotives' drive movement.

M. Baldwin, USA (Pennsylvania): improvement of the locomotive.

Wilhelm Engerth, Austria: improvement of the mountain locomotive, 1851.

Nikolaus Riggenbach: cog wheel patent, 1863.

Haardy, Augsburg: design of vacuum brakes.

J. Haag, Augsburg: design of system for steam heating.

H. Lilliehöök, Sweden: improvement of Haag's system.

E. Storckenfeldt, Sweden: improvement of the heating system.

Haberlein: improvement of friction brakes.

George Westinghouse, USA: design of air brakes, 1869.

Patrick Stirling, Scotland: design of the drivewheel, 1870.

Richardson and Turner, USA: design of the slide valve.

William Stroudley, England (Brighton): design of internal cylinders, 1882.

Fried (Krupp) Essen: improvement of axles and wheels.

Guiseppe Zara, Italy: improvement of the steam locomotive, 1900.

Krauss and Helmholz: improvement of the bogie system.

Axel Carlquist, Sweden: improvement of the piston slide valve.

K. J. Mellin, resident of USA: improvement of ventilating system.

Werner Siemens: design of current supplied by a third rail.

The names mentioned are very clearly documented in, for example, *The State Railways* 1856-1906. Techno-economic Writings," Edited by Gustav Welin.

Besides Pullman in Chicago these apply to enterprises such as:

Air Brake, New York
Beyer, Peacock, Manchester
Borsig, Berlin
Brown and Marshall, Birmingham
Eisenbahnbedarf, Berlin
Haag, Augsburg
Krauss, Munich
Lauenstein, Hamburg
Luke-Hofman, Breslau
Maffei, Munich
Maschinenbau, Nurenberg
Norddeutsche, Berlin
Richard Locomotive Works, USA
Sharp and Stewart, Manchester
Vickers, Sheffield

The enterprises in this line of business in Sweden are these:
Motala Manufacturing Co. 1859 (1822).

Kockums Mechanical Mfg. Co. Malmö, 1859 (1840).
Car Manufacturing, Liljeholmen, 1860.
P. I. Ekman, Kungsholms Machine Factory, 1862.
Alexander Keiller & Co., Göteborg, 1863 (1841, 1858, 1867).
Nydqvist & Holm Co., Trollhättan, 1866 (1847).
Norrköpings Mechanical Mfg. Co. 1875.
Atlas Company, Stockholm, 1876.
ASEA, Västerås, 1883.
Ljunggrens Mfg. Co., Kristinehamn, 1894.
Car Fabricators Co., Södertälje, 1897.
Hesselholms Mechanical Mfg. Co., 1900.
Kalmar Mfg. Co., 1902.
Rössels Mechanical Mfg. Co., 1903, later moved to Arlöfs and in ASJ, 1918.
Swedish Railway car Factory, Linköping, 1907

The Manufacture of Railway Cars

I have taken the following as a general background to my earlier section on Pullman and I would like to continue with a description of some Swedish workshops that made railway cars of wood. The reason for this is naturally that the Swedish carpenters at Pullman worked in shops of a similar kind, and I approach the makers of railway cars, first at Pullman and thereafter in Sweden, for comparison. It is important to note that the producers of cars in wood followed the footsteps of the Swedish carpenters at Pullman.

Thanks to Mrs. Duane Doty we have a description of the manufacture of railroad cars at Pullman from the year 1893, and as a starting point I will quote from it.   [in English]

> A visitor at the Pullman works often notices carloads of newly-rolled rod and bar iron of various sizes, which are awaiting some of the many transformations to fit it for manifold uses in cars. In the bolt works rods are cut to suitable lengths and headed and threaded for the many varieties of bolts used. In the blacksmith shop and in the hammer shop flat bars are made into the various forms required in trucks and car bodies. This merchantable iron, rolled with the greatest accuracy, comes from the Pullman Iron and Steel Works, which is situated on the west shore of Lake Calumet and on the south side of One Hundred and Seventh street extended. The work at this rolling mill is all done on the first or ground floor. The size of the original building was 177 feet by 194 feet, to which has been added a frame extension 137 by 36 feet in size, making in all 39,270 square feet, or nearly an acre of floor space for the machinery of the mills. Fully as much space is occupied outside by sheds and grounds for storage of scrap iron. This mill, when in operation presents a busy scene and one of unusual interest to the spectator. Two hundred and fifty men are employed, and at some seasons the works have to run night and day. The iron here is made from scrap, such as old rails, worn-out car axles, and, in fact, almost every form of scrap iron collected. Many thousand tons of this scrap may always be seen at the mill.
>
> The glass department cuts the glass, etches it and silvers it when required, and makes and finishes all the mirrors. When everything is ready, the prepared materials are delivered as needed at the compartments where the cars are to be erected. First the bottom materials such as sills, floor joists, flooring draft timbers and transoms, arrive and are taken in hand by the bottom-builders.
>
> After a careful inspection the car is taken by the outside painters, and is entered at the same time by the inside finishers, who put in and finish the nice inside woodwork, which is of the best kinds of lumber, such as oak, ash, cherry, mahogany, or vermilion. The piping for heating and for lighting is set in before the seats are placed in position. The inside finish too, conceals the electric wires which may be called for in the specifications. Cars are lighted by oil, gas, or electricity.
>
> When the inside woodwork is all in place, and some of this finish comprises exquisite carving, the inside painters go over the entire interior woodwork, making the car ready for the trimmers, who place the bronze or plated trimmings upon doors, sash blinds and walls. The upholstering, draperies, seat coverings, carpets,

etc., which have all been previously prepared, are now put in, and when the finishing touches are added by the equipment department, the car is ready for delivery to its purchaser, to whom it is sometimes sent by special messenger.

Mrs. Duane Doty, *The Town of Pullman*, 1893 (1974) p. 146ff.

But thanks to Mrs. Duane Doty's writings about the Swedish carpenters' work, the types of wood used by the carpenters at Pullman are of particular interest. She reports that they used oak from Arkansas and Indiana, fir from Michigan and Wisconsin, maple and poplar from Michigan and Indiana, elm from Illinois and Ohio, birch from Michigan and Wisconsin, ash from Indiana and Michigan, cedar wood from California and New Jersey, cherry wood from Indiana and Michigan, and mahogany from Mexico and Honduras.

The timber was stored in the big lumber yards. Between 175 and 215 men worked there, of which 9/10ths were Hollanders [from Roseland]. About 300 cars were always there in readiness to transport material to the right workplace.

Marble for the wash stand trimming was taken from Tennessee, but in particular cases, from Italy.

By 1893, 35,000 passenger cars had been built and were rolling on America's rails. A single such vehicle would cost between 5,000 and 10,000 dollars. Production was prepared from drawings of every detail that indicated quality and size, painting and finishing.

Comparison with corresponding industries in Sweden

The well known car industry in the town of Lijeholm was established for the preparation and upkeep of rolling stock in 1860. It consisted of locomotive shop, smithy, and car shop.

Steam engines and boilers (already displayed in the Stockholm Exhibition of 1866) were manufactured at Bolinder's factory in Stockholm.

In 1869 this car shop's size was 2674 square meters and it consisted of a metal foundry, wheel repair shop, wheel turning shop, smithy with 8 hearths, wire and machine shops with 17 different shop machines, locomotive shop with 83 switch tracks and five pits of 12.3 meters each, and also watchmen and a gate keeper's residence. Sheet metal work was done in the locomotive works. The buildings were constructed with walls of brick; the roof trusses of wood and iron and the outer roofs of iron plating on wood panels. Plank and earth floors and floors of stone tiles were interchanged with concrete. The overhead traverse crane had been supplied by the Ludvigberg factory in Stockholm. The lighting was done by gas. Water was pumped from Årstaviken to the cisterns. Upholsterers were transferred from Liljeholm to the Tomteboda car shops in 1899. Electrification was done at the beginning of September, 1898, and generators were purchased from ASEA. The labor force consisted of about 320 persons.

The car shops at Liljeholm in Stockholm were designed for short cars. After the introduction of bogie cars larger shops were needed. One such was at Tomteboda, which was built in 1898-1900; others were in Göteborg, Malmö, Örebro, Motala, Kristinehamn, Östersund, Bollnäs, Svartön in Luleå, and Boden.

The shops at Tomteboda consisted of the offices, machine shop, electric power station, upholstery shop, smithy, sheet metal shop, boiler and machine room, car shop, painting shop, carpenter shop, gate keeper's house, supply room, store, and cook house. The car shop itself was fitted out with planers, wheel turners, lathes, plate shears, bench shears, boring machines, plate roller, grinding machines, filing benches, threading machines motors, grindstones and washing basins The departments were heated from the steam boiler room.

In Göteborg factories already appear on Gullbergs point in 1858 in the earliest drawings of A. W. Edelsvärd the same architect that we met with when we were dealing with the workers' dwellings at

Klippan. In 1884 the workplace in Göteborg consisted of office premises, machine shop, locomotive works, plate workshop, forge, copper mill, boiler and machine house, foundry, car shop, painting shop, carpenter shop, and boiler tube repair shop. In the metal shop were places for five locomotive boilers at the same time. Bogie car manufacturing had up to 50 meters of interconnecting tracks.

Carpenter and paint shops were in their turn equipped with lathes, milling machines, boring machines, planing machines, threading machines, shear and punch machines, traction engines, circular saws, crosscut saws, bandsaws, mortising machines, planer-jointer, wood lathe, plate aligning machine, babbitt sinker, grindstones, circular tables, filing benches, buffer presses, drying ovens, steam cookers, steam boilers, gas meters, stoves, lockers, tool supplies, floor cranes, gas pipes, generators or motors, arc lamps, and washing basins. The cranes had been supplied by Th. Dunn & Co., Manchester. Heating was done by steam and stoves. The cylinder boring machines were obtained from Capitaine in Frankfurt, the planing machines from Mayer & Schmidt in Offenbach, the wheel turners from The Pond Machine Tool Co., the locomotive wheel turners from Beyer & Peacock, cranes from ASEA in Västerås.

The workers were divided in shifts at each base and over these was a foreman. The foremen in their turn received their instructions from the supervisor. These again were accountable to the machine director. The work shift came to 10 hours and for control a metal plate stamped with the worker's number was used. Central Control was at the main factory in Stockholm. Safety devices consisted of first aid cabinets.

I first presented the section about the workplace, machines, tools, work methods, and work conditions in my writings in *National Railroads* 1856-1906, page 376ff.

The impact of the railroads has been discussed by countless authors. Åke Holmberg for example has, in his *World History II,* 1982, expressed it in this way, page 178:

> It is something to think about, that this was possibly the 19th Century's greatest accomplishment in world history. In 1869 the first connection across the whole continent (USA) was completed. During the one single decade of 1880, 75,000 miles of railroad were realized—seven times the Swedish railroad network at its longest.

On the part of Sweden, Lars-Arne Norborg wrote in *Swedish Public Development 1809-1979,* 1980 p. 41, that when the Swedish railroad network of 1850-1880 was built under the direction of Nils Ericson, care was taken to improve the transportation possibilities for industrial products as well as raw materials and that industry's location possibilities were broadened at the same time as provision was created for machines, spare parts and repairs.

The railroad stations attracted shops, service functions, and small industry. Communities of a new type outside the surrounding farming community were developed (for example in Eslöv, Hässleholm, Nässjö, Katrineholm). "Here the high-born, priests, and big farmers did not dominate the small entrepreneurs, lower servants, and laborers. Therefore the station communities became the center for peoples' movements and democratizing efforts."

"The Railroad City"

Douglas C. North, in his well-known review of American economic history, *Growth and Welfare in the American Past,* 1996, p. 86, stresses that the railroads' greatest achievement is that they enabled the reduction of transportation costs; and that they promoted the development of other manufacturing sectors as the demand for iron, machines, and wood products increased.

This in its turn allowed several export sectors a financial capability from which came the import of capital goods. The expansion of railroads to every corner of the USA was one of the most dramatic events of the 19th Century. The solution of the complex problem of railroad expansion demanded an enormous organization and immense investments.

In a recent work by Marco d'Eramo, *Das Schwein und der Wolkenkrazer,*[2] 1977, he calls Chicago "the city of railroads" with its "colossal stream of goods" on the Northern Pacific, Chicago Burlington and Quincy, Northwestern, and Illinois Central lines. He even used the word, "railroad republic" for "the windy city." It was really not likely, with the unreasonable number of track miles and engines and car yards in constantly increasing numbers, that every line could claim its own railroad station, buildings of all types, tunnels, bridges, and water reservoirs. Such facilities were shared by many lines.

Suddenly, many people were coming every day. For over 100 million Americans Chicago was only "a night train away." Germans, Irish, Swedes, Poles, Italians, Indians, and black and yellow; all came to the city in passenger coaches. And that didn't mean that merchandise, corn, and meat were not widely transported in freight cars to the hungry city dwellers, writes d'Eramo in his graphic manner.

In 1868, a merchant, George H. Hammond, from Detroit, invented the first refrigerator car (filled with ice). Ice houses were built along the railroad lines, and thousands of men brought ice out of Lake Michigan; but in 1872 the first cars cooled with ammonia compressors were built, which in one blow caused these ice men to be unemployed.

Phillip Armour, who was head of his meat packing empire created the motto: "We feed the world". page 46. Animals were imported from Illinois, Iowa, Kentucky, and Indiana although Texas was known for the best horned cattle. (A successor to his empire today is McDonald's and Quaker Oats.") The slaughter houses and sausage makers employed about 30,000 around the turn of the century, 1900, and the meat packing industry 46,000.

Eight million immigrants came to the USA between 1840 and 1880 and 24 million between 1880 and 1930. In the first period they were in fact from Great Britain, Ireland, Scandinavia, and Germany. In the other period most originated from East and South Europe.

Marco d'Eramo is a sociologist from Rome who studied with Pierre Bourdieu in Paris, and in this book about Chicago which has the sub-title, "Chicago. A History of Our Future," he has many good characterizations. For example: [in German]

If America is the holy land of capitalism, then Chicago is its Jerusalem, page 16.

The application of mathematics to hogs, page 21.

A scraper of the heavens [skyscraper] page 62

Balloon frame houses, page 83.

Chicago, the world capital of the lumber markets, page 90.

Suburban paradise, page 170.

In ancient times they said all roads led to Rome; in modern times all railroads lead to Chicago, page 153.

Chicago, the Marseille of our Mediterranean, page 155.

The Italians, the Chinese, the Orient, page 163.

Labor market according to nationalities, page 167.

The problem of Irish servant girls, page 168.

Chicago with its stinking slaughter houses, its smoking factories and sooty railroads, among its thousand nationalities and languages, page 169.

The modern crime syndicate, page 170.

Discrimination in the sleeping cars, page 194.

Most of these characterizations speak clearly for themselves, but here follows a supplement.

The architects of the skyscrapers belong to an admirable group. They are: Dankmar Adler, Daniel H. Burnham, John W. Root, William Le Baron Jenny, Louis Sullivan, Frank Lloyd Wright, William

Holabird, and Henry Hobson Richardson. Skeletons of Bessemer steel had been put to use in 1883 during the rebuilding after the fire of 1871, and the skyscrapers' images resemble fossilized dinosaurs when one sees their contours by night. Pages 62-63.

He saw the "lumber people" flooding Chicago in the late autumn [after the fire] with their products and their axes and saws and their liquidity problem. Later they withdrew farther north to the forests and the coldness. They went forth like a whirlwind through Wisconsin, Michigan, and Minnesota, but they also built everything–houses, schools, offices, and churches. Page 91. The horse trams ran between Chicago and its suburbs with all their idyllic names; their trees, woods, and gardens. Thanks to the trains, people could now live far from their places of employment (70,000 commuters in the year 1880), page 112, and the town of Pullman had a line into The Loop. Because of Henry Ford's Model-T in 1908 individuals began to attain freedom, but such an acquisition required a whole 25 month's salary for a worker. In 1925 he only needed to use three, a remarkable showing. page 121. As to the line, "Discrimination in the sleeping cars," the matter was treated by George M. Pullman, and was handled with understanding.

Pullman had with foresight established his factory and workers' homes at the shore of Lake Calumet. This influenced the movement of Chicago steel mills. Originally they lay immediately north of Chicago's "downtown" but toward the close of the century the owners moved to the spaces on the Calumet River, near the Indiana state line.

Marco d'Eramo asserted, however, that Pullman had always had luck, for had he not gotten the assignment in 1865 to arrange for the transportation of President Lincoln's remains, and all those associated, between Chicago and Springfield, his plans for "The Pioneer" might not have been successful. Orders were given for the widening of platforms, bridges, and tunnels and thereby the bigger, more comfortable, luxurious cars could roll on the tracks. The advantages were obvious and they came to be followed throughout most parts of America, page 195. The situation had an impetus, and four years later 48 sleeping cars were already on the rails, followed by restaurant cars and salon cars. Pullman now had his own employees working on trains and his own fabrication and repair shops. Marco d'Eramo was among those who supposed that Pullman was inspired by Sir Titus Salt with Saltair–an industrial community in England and by Krupp in Essen, when he settled on Lake Calumet, 20 miles south of "The Loop" in 1880, and built his factory there. Page 196.

We now leave Marco d'Eramo after having established that the Italian sociologist, like a detective, examined the history of Chicago and cleverly characterized parts of it.

And here this chapter approaches its end, but first I will return to Pullman and tie it to Ernst Åkerberg in Pullman, where I left him in 1905. Thanks go to his nephew who, in September 1997, sent some letters that he had earlier traced and recovered.

Åkerberg–Carpenters, second and third generations

The year is now 1906, when Ernest, as he began to call himself then, and Helene Hellstrom are married. The wedding took place in Roseland on Friday, September 14th. In the wedding party was brother-in-law A. M. Benander, married to Helene's older sister, Hulda (born 8/24/1864 and emigrated to Chicago in 1889). The wedding was described at great length in the congregation newspaper's fall edition, 1906, under the headline "Other events." The report particularly stressed that the bride's elderly father, Carl Hellström, miller from Ryfors Bruk, had "submitted to the difficulties of the journey with his beloved child and thereby made acquaintance with a multitude of grandchildren." In addition to all the family in Pullman and Roseland, the congregation's board members were invited.

> First rate organ music appropriate for the occasion was presented by the congregation's organist Arvid Gylling and the choir graced the occasion with well-performed song. After the festivities ended in the church,

the whole party repaired to the lower room, where the happy bridal couple received hearty congratulations and wishes of happiness. After which, all were seated at a tastefully laid and decorated table. After speeches and songs and reading of telegrams from Mullsjö the newlyweds departed to their new residence.

The lines quoted above inform us that the Okerbergs acquired a better residence in 1906.

Helene and Ernest had their first child in 1907, a son, Arnold; Albert then followed in 1910, Kenneth in 1916, and Margaret, called Peggy, in 1920. Of these, only Margaret is now living.

In 1922 they bought their own house, and in a photo Ernest sits with his sons Kenneth and Albert and happily peers at Helene who is taking the picture. Ernest wears his Sunday clothes, tie, and straw hat. Albert has a sport cap and Kenneth, a little child's hat.

Letters saved from 11/10 and 11/17/1912, and also from 08/10/1923 and 02/01/1928 show how things went for the family later. In 1912 Ernest made a visit "home" to Ryfors for four months. It was an uncertain thing whether he would get his job back when he returned, but he was lucky. After the Ryfors visit he associated with a Benson family at 2820 Racine Ave., related to Ida Ljungblad, Barnarpsgatan 11 in Jönköping. Through Reinhold Hurtig they also knew Elisabeth Söderman, who lived with her uncle Kurt Karlsson in Chicago. "We were invited there for supper, where we talked a lot about Sweden, and about Ryfors in particular. Yes, how fine it is that a man does not forget dear old Sweden so easily! There are many I would have liked to visit there but I didn't have enough time."

When Helene wrote to her in-laws in 1912 she told them that Arnold had begun Sunday school again in Pullman.

In 1923 the whole family was invited to Helene's brother Reinhold's who had bought a summer cottage at Lake Geneva, Wisconsin, and there they fished and swam. The rest of the time Ernest worked very hard. "In Pullman you can't work the way some of the carpenters in Ryfors used to work. I remember they took it so easy and went home for coffee and food three or four times a day. They didn't know how good they really had it in Ryfors."

On July 15, 1923 all the Ryfors members in the club went on a picnic, and afterwards Helene closed her letter to her sister-in-law in this way: "The assembly gathered in Washington Park this time, and it was here that Fingal Hillstrom's poem, *Memories of Ryfors* was presented. That afternoon our President, Warren G. Harding was buried. Factories were closed everywhere."

1928 was a cold winter on Lake Michigan; many were unemployed and "everything was so expensive. Ernest has worked steadily for a few weeks lately," wrote Helene in another letter to her in-laws and continued, "But we suffer no need when we have our health."

We have further information about the families' lives through a few photographs, one of Ernest from 1944 in which he sits on the front bumper of his new-looking car. It is taken in front of their house, and Ernest has just taken his pension at the age of 65. And another of Ernest and the three sons, also taken in the 1940s. I got them from Ernest's grandson, Paul Okerberg, a resident of Charleston, South Carolina, together with an e-mail of 07/14/1997. Here Paul informs us:

[In English] Ernest worked for 43 years at Pullman and was so respected for his work and leadership that Pullman had wanted him to come back right after he retired. Ernest did not go back, saying that he had enough.

The Swedish immigrants were valued not only for their reputation as hard workers, but also the quality of their work and artistry.

Ernest did not get paid by the hour, but was compensated by how many sleeper cars were completed. This was called piecework and was a real hardship since unless things were completed there was no pay to support his family.

On 02/07/1998 I also received information on the history of the Hillstrom family in the second and third generations through D. Armour Hillstrom of Charlottesville, Virginia, a son of David Hillstrom.

The miller Karl Alfred Hellstrom of Sagers at Ryfors and his wife Helena, born Sjöberg, had eleven children, eight sons and three daughters between the years 1858-1881. All emigrated to Chicago with the three eldest in the lead, John, Edward and Oscar, and they found work at the Pullman Car Works. In his turn their younger brother was encouraged to leave Ryfors and as soon as he came they also helped him to work at Pullman. One of these, Armour's father, had learned to be a master carpenter in Jönköping.

> [in English] "Dad worked on the beautiful interior trim of the Pullman sleeping cars. Handsome and exotic woods from Africa and around the world were used. He said he had to be so careful when sanding these expensive woods because you could easily sand right through the veneer and into the wood backing, and that meant trouble. Lolita, Mr. Pullman's daughter[3] had the sinecure of naming each new Pullman sleeper at a nice salary."

Fritiof advanced to Inspector at Pullman. Oscar, in the latter part of his life, owned his own mortgage business in the town of Pullman. John went to work in a real estate office. Phillip moved to the West Coast, developed his musical talent and became a choral director. Fingal Hillstrom, as we have seen, was responsible for the songs in the Ryfors Club. He was not only a choral director but also made his own arrangements of the Psalms and Swedish choral songs.

David founded his own successful enterprise in the steel business, The Corry Jamestown corp. Only Pontus of the eleven siblings returned to Sweden and continued after his father as a miller in Sörarps Mill at Ryfors.

In the rounding off of this chapter with its main theme of the production of railroad cars, I have had help from Wolfgang Schivelbusch. In his book on the history of railroad travel and of the times of industrialization in the 1880 decade, he describes the building of railroads in the USA; that they let the railroad cars operate in adverse weather to save costs; when land was cheap but there was a scarcity of manpower. Even if the roadbeds were uneven the cars went just as easily and softly thanks to the so-called bogie, where the basket at each end rested on a turnable wheel rack with a short axle distance while in England they continued to use two-axle passenger cars. In Europe the idea of the compartment system had been taken from stage coaches while the American version was taken from river boat salons.

In the USA the railroad train was a kind of rolling vessel where, thanks to G. M. Pullman, passengers could both eat and sleep. (See Göran Sjögård's review of Schivelbusch in *Rig* 1986, nr. 1, page 26ff.) In the luxurious Pullman salon cars the passengers acquired "a new experience," an unobstructed view when the sleeping partitions were removed, which induced first and second class passengers to read during the train journey and, according to Schivelbusch, forced them to sit with other people without initiating conversation. Third and fourth class passengers, however, entertained themselves with lively conversation.

Here ends this chapter which began with "All Railroads Lead to Chicago," and continued with chosen sections within our technical field of knowledge. The predominant motivation was a wish to give an overview and a model. (The research is, of course, self-initiated and guides this investigation.)

[1] All railroads lead to Chicago

[2] Hogs and Skyscrapers

[3] No daughter of G. M. Pullman named Lolita can be found in known sources.

The following is from a publication titled, *Memorandum of Information,* issued by The Pullman Company on February 17, 1947:

Since 1865, when the "Pioneer"–the first sleeping car built by George M. Pullman–went into service, Pullman cars have borne distinctive names: Westchester county, Nob Hill, James Monroe, Jenny Lind, and Squaw Bonnet....Across the nation these names have rolled, year after year in endless procession. Seen by lantern light at a whistle stop, or in the glare of Grand Central Station, these and thousands of other Pullman car names have captured the public's imagination and interest and have become part of our folklore of American business. They are an American institution.

These names generally, but not always, indicate the different types of accommodations offered by the specific cars–parlor cars bear the names of flowers and birds, observation cars have names preceded by "Mt." or "Mountain," ten section, two drawing room cars are named "Points," and so on.

Seasoned travelers recognize individual Pullman cars by their names, greet them as old friends when they meet again and again in scattered sections of the country. Thousands of words in the press and magazines have been written about Pullman cars' names. And there has been much speculation and endless rumor about the sources of names and the identity of the persons who provide the names.

Locomotive 157. Picture in R. R. Roman's Geschichte der Eisenbahn, (Story of Railroads), *1977.*

Before Pullman in an American passenger car, 1852. From Oliver Jensen, Railroads in America, *1975, p. 23.*

*Production of passenger cars in Pullman factory, 1880.
From John H. White, The American Railroad Passenger Car, 1978, p. 437.*

Ernest Åkerberg, 1944. Photo owned by Tage Åkerberg.

Ernest Åkerberg and his three sons, Arnold, Kenneth and Albert, 1941. Owned by Tage Åkerberg.

Ernest Åkerberg's grandson, Paul Okerberg with his son, Joshua. From the Marietta Daily Journal, *11/13/1989.*

Chapter IX
My Conclusion

My descriptions in eight chapters about Pullman in Chicago, from which selected parts of the town and the workers' stories are described based on the Swedes' achievements, now come to a conclusion.

In the Time. It happened in that part of the 19th century when railroads extended all over the world. Åke Holmberg writes that it might really be considered the 19th century's greatest historical achievement. In the USA the first connection across the whole continent was already completed in 1869, and all this during the previous decade. The 19th century produced 75,000 miles of railroads–seven times the Swedish network at its longest. The Swedish rail network was developed between 1850-1880 under the leadership of Nils Ericson and the transport possibilities were widened at the same time the demand for machinery, spare parts, and repairs was created.

Railroad stations spawned shops, service functions, and small industries. A new type of society became the center for folk movements and democratic aspirations.

Also in America the spreading of the railroads to every corner of the USA was considered one of the most dramatic events of the 19th century. Douglas C. North stressed in his great overview of American economic history that the very greatest significance was in the railroads having made lower transportation costs possible, and perhaps above all, that the railroads had created an enormous organization and unprecedented investments. Railroad researchers Robert Fogel in *Railroads and American Economic Growth,* 1964, page 218ff and Albert Fishlow in *American Railroads and the Transformation of the Antebellum Economy,* 1971, page 63ff, have, on the other hand, maintained that it is nowhere demonstrated that the railroads created an absolute condition for the industrial emergence.

A third American railroad researcher, Albro Martin has in every circumstance assigned G.M. Pullman a leading role. This occurs in the chapter, "The Era of Modern Passenger Trains Begins in 1870," in the book with the compelling title, *Railroads Triumphant,* 1922.

In the place. The thought came to me in 1987 to write about Pullman; of the renowned products produced in its factories, of its remarkable town plan and its thoroughly planned architecture, of the situation concerning the world's exposition in 1893, and of the ingenuity of George Mortimer Pullman and his ability to unite several of the most skillful planners and architects. And from there to the place of Swedes who obtained work there in that most successful industry; the dwellings equipped with all conveniences, and situated in a carefully planned town with trees, planting, and lawns; with two lakes and a canal; with access to shops, restaurants, sports facilities and baths!

During the Colombian Exposition, this town of Pullman received an award for its cleanliness and healthfulness.

The idea of writing about it grew from my study of the town of Pullman during the time I was commissioned to draw up general outlines for the proposed Swedish American Museum on North Clark Street in Andersonville, Chicago. I suggested it should be a Swedish-American center with a permanent exhibit and with possibilities for occasional exhibits, where other ethnic groups could be invited to show their history. In view of that, Göteborg, in its role of sister city to Chicago could perhaps make a contribution with current elements from Sweden and the rest of the North.

Socially, Pullman had certainly been a renowned model community up to 1894, when it was alleged that it was also a community of serfs where the inhabitants were bound to their workplace. After compulsory arbitration was ruled by the highest court in Illinois, the tenants who remained in the town gradually became owners of the row houses.

The unfavorable publicity that followed all the earlier eulogies, convinced many industrialists that the corporate city after the Pullman model was simply no longer desirable.

Just as John W. Reps showed in *The making of Urban America,* 1965, page 424, more were nevertheless planned, such as Barberton, Ohio in 1891 by the architect W. A. Johnston on Lake Anna (after Barber's daughter) with a central green built at the side reminiscent of the town of Pullman. Likewise, in the year 1893, Granite City, Illinois near the Mississippi River, where the company built the first houses but then offered them for sale. And Vandergriff, Pennsylvania, northeast of Pittsburgh, built in a loop of the Kiskimineta River. Here the Apollo Iron and Steel company commissioned the firm of Frederick Law Olmsted and John Charles Olmsted to create a new town for workers and the factory. I mentioned the elder Olmsted in my earlier study of New Britain, Connecticut, 1988, page 23ff. The plan for Vandergrift, Reps believes, "shows little of the genius that marked the best residential plans of Fredrick L. Olmsted."

Lasse Brunnström and Mats Ahnlund, in their study of 1987, also contended that New England's factory communities could be counted among the very early model communities. They named, among others, South Manchester, Connecticut, Hopedale, Massachusetts, and Peace Dale, Rhode Island, page 20. As to Sweden, it appears that earlier information more closely defined and borrowed from Swedish model communities, states that much discussion of prototype factories and industrial communities had been the inspiration for the Swedish welfare state which developed during the Twentieth Century, Page 46.

A good many years have now passed since my project in Chicago in the fall of 1987. The Swedish American Museum has, under its director, General Consul Kerstin Lane, been developed with success. Since that time I have had much additional information, but the thought of writing my impressions of Pullman has remained, and I have privately resumed my research concerning it.

And now, consequently, the work stands with impressions—of mine and of others, with pictures old and new, and with questions answered and unanswered.

Earlier, I quoted from Anita R. Olson's 1990 assessment of Swedes in Chicago in 1880-1920; how they felt that their situation dynamics were comparable with their experience in Sweden and felt themselves more Swedish here than at home, and how they adapted themselves to city life. My own impression of Swedes in Pullman is that they truly helped to form the culture of this town, and that in different ways they established their presence—there in the row houses, during working hours, and in their free time.

During my final revisions of this chapter, I made contact, through Anders Jarlert, with Ingvar Dahlbacka of Åbo, and his treatise from 1994 of how a Finnish community had become Americanized in New York City. Altogether it might be established that there were no sharp boundaries between different ethnic groups within their respective regions of investigation, but that they alternately on different levels brought themselves closer to their American surroundings.

The communities became assembly places for new immigrants where they could meet their own countrymen, get some news from home, visit in their own mother tongue, and celebrate church services in Swedish. English, naturally enough, first took its foothold among the younger age groups, for whom the English services had greater drawing power. For the respective congregations, the bonds to the regions of origin in Sweden are kept alive through the years. The older generation is kept bound to the traditions of the homeland to a great extent, while the younger generation, reared in the USA, prefers to cling to those traditions more American. In one respect, however, we have come to different conclusions, and it applies to name giving. Ingvar Dahlbacka in his investigation has found, in contrast to mine, a strong American influence (p. 144, ff). It was even stronger, of course, in the beginning of the period of investigation. This holds true when the fathers were not able to find some integration in the American surroundings and there were not many mixed marriages. Many little groups could be observed within the congregational framework. These were well-defined, as we saw in Chapter 3.

Together, Dahlbacka and I have found that the congregations in themselves have not exhibited any outstanding qualities. They were formed and were changed substantially during the years, but they did provide a center for fellowship both on weekdays and Sundays. Access to the church's social room and kitchen especially, functioned for meaningful contacts with Americans and other ethnic groups in the neighborhoods. Ingvar Dahlbacka characterizes the general adjustment processes as cautious and optimistic within his congregation in New York, which, of course, Raymond E. Johnson also found in Pullman.

To clarify the actual situation in Chicago and Pullman, I will cite some verses from Carl Sandburg (1878-1967) *Chicago,* and Artur Lundkvist (1906-1991) *Sandburg's America.* Both are unsurpassed in portraying with sensitivity and thought, some of the feelings as they may have been felt at the time.

Hog Butcher for the world
Tool Maker, Stacker of Wheat,
Player with Railroads and the Nation's Freight Handler;
Stormy, husky, brawling,
City of the Big Shoulders:

      Sandburg

I come from the corn prairies
from the morning-red mountains and the evening-blue valleys
From the cities, roads, rivers, timber woods—
I bend over the typewriter
and fling down Chicago's raucous laugh.

      Lundqvist

Finally: What an experience it must have been around the turn of the century, 1900, for the Swedish farm boy from the region west of Vättern to come to Pullman and to Chicago; and what an experience it is around the turn of the century, 2000, to come to the town of Pullman! It is participation in an important past; of belching chimneys and whirling wheels; and we witness now a cultural inheritance which is preserved—truly a world's cultural inheritance.

Sometimes the time and scope of my investigations have been protracted; sometimes they have been expanded; but above all, it is the families Åkerberg and Johnson that have given a human face to my story.

They are accomplished studies in which several intertwined trails have consequently been found:

Pullman in Chicago, which has its continuation in the preserved object, Pullman;

The emigrants from Ryfors, who came from a region characterized by traditions, and in their new situation at Pullman, met a touchy situation.

What principally held them together was the stabilizing social community which the family relationships provided.

Feelings of solidarity found expression in gathering around the accordion on a Saturday afternoon. Oscar Karlsson from Göteborg plays the accordion for his companions, several of whom are newly arrived. Dreams of a better life. The photo from around 1920 belongs to Bolla Erikson.

The clock tower in 1938. On December 1st, 1998, the building was ravaged by fire at the hands of an arsonist. Photo by Warren Johnson.

Sources, Periodicals, Literature

Sources
Informants:
Åke Axell, Mullsjö
Bengt Berglund, Göteborg
Stanley Buder, New York
Woodrow Eisenhart, Chicago, IL
Janice Helge, South Holland, IL
Nils Hellström, Ryfors
D. Armour Hillstrom, Charlottsville, VA
Mike C. Hillstrom, Oak Brook, IL
Raymond E. Johnson, Westminster, CO
Ingemar Lindstrand, Linköping
Ulf Smedbo, Göteborg
Paul Okerberg, Charleston, SC
Tage Åkerberg, Anneberg

Informants who answered my inquiry
Historic Pullman Foundation, HPF, Chicago, IL
Newberry Library, Chicago, Pullman Collection
South Suburban Genealogical and Historical Society, SSGHS, South Holland, IL
Chicago Historical Society, Chicago, IL
Manuscript collections, picture archives, and map collection.
Swedish Emigration Institute, Växjö
Chicago Ministerial Acts
Sweden's Railway Museum, Gävle
The following searched on the internet:
Search code: Pullman, Chicago, Railroad.
Inquiries answered: 413.

Periodicals

Bekänneren
The Carbuilder
Luther Banéret
Harper's Monthly
Højskolebladet
Ny Illustrerad Tidning
Prärieblomman
Pullman Journal
Pullman News
Svenska Amerikanaren
Tribunen

The Greater Roseland Area of Chicago
Tåg, Svenska Järnvägsklubbens Tidning

Literature

Ahnlund, Mats-Brunnström, Lasse
Från Dawson till Pullman, Nordamerikanska bolagssamhällen–en översikt. I:Bebyggelsehistorisk tidskrift 1987,nr.3.

Ahrén, Herman, red.,
Nylycke socken, En hembygdsbok, 1955

Allén, Sture–Wåhlin, Staffan
Förnamnsboken. De 10.000 vanligaste förnamnen, 1995

Arvastson, Gösta
Maskinmänniskan, 1987

Barton, H. Arnold
A Folk Divided, Homeland Swedes and Swedish Americans, 1840-1940, 1994

Behrend, George
Pullman in Europe, 1962

Beijbom, Ulf
Amerika, En bok om utvandrigen, 1977

Beijbom Ulf, ed.
Swedes in America, New Perspectives, 1993

Beijbom Ulf
Swedes in Chicago, A demographic and social study of the 1846-1880 immigration, 1971

Berger, J. V.
Vår kyrka, de svensk-amerikanska kyrkliga förhållandena, sedda från nationell och folklig synpunkt, 1912

Berglund, Bengt
Industriklassens formulering. Arbete och teknisk förändring vid tre svenska fabriker under 1800 talet, 1982

Blanck, Dag-Runblom, Harald
Swedish Life in American Cities, 1991

Blanck, Dag
Becoming Swedish-American, 1997

Bluestone, Daniel
Contracting Chicago, 1991

Bringéus, Nils-Arvid
Människan som kulturvarelse, 1986

Buder, Stanley
An Experiment in Industrial Order and Community Planning 1880-1930, 1967

Carling Henrik
Fra Amerika, 1897

Cornell, Elias
De stora utställningarnas arkitekturhistoria, 1952
Cultural and urban Aspects of an Immigrant People 1850-1930, 1981

Curman, Johan
Entreprenören C.F. Lundström 1823-1917, En tidtig europé, 1996

Dahlbacka, Ingvar
Svensk-finska Evangelisk-lutherska församlingen av New York City 1919-1935, 1994. En finlandssvensk
    emigrantförsamling amerikaniseras, 1994

Darley, Gillian
Villages of Vision, 1975

Daun, Åke
Den europeiska identiteten Bidrag till samtal om Sveriges framtid, 1992

De Geer, Eric
Emigrationen i Västsverige i slutet av 1880-talet I Ymer 1957, s. 194-223

Doty, Mrs. Duane
The Town of Pullman. Its Growth with Brief Accounts of its Industries 1974, 1990

Dickson, Walter
Amerika, 1954

Ek, Sven B.
Qltur som problem, 1989

d'Eramo, Marco
Das Schwien und der Wolkenkrazer. Chicago und der Zukunft, 1997

Fishlow, A.
American Railroads and the Transformation of the Ante bellum Economy, 1971

Fogel, R.
Railroads and American Economic Growth, 1946

Giddens, Anthony
The Consequences of Modernity, 1990

Gullberg, Gustaf
Boken om Chicago–snabbmålningar från en resa till verldsutställningen, 1892, 1893

Hammar, Hugo
Som emigrant i USA, 1938

Hamilton, Ellis C.
Boken om tåg, 1975

Hayden, Doleres
Seven American Utopias, 1976

Heckscher, Eli F.
Till belysning av järnvägarnas betydelse för Sveriges ekonomiska utveckling, 1907

Henricson, Ingvar-Lindblad, Hans
Tur och retur Amerika, 1995

Holbrook, Stewart H.
The Story of American Railroads, 1947

Holmberg, Åke
Världshistoria, 2, 1882

Isacson, Maths-Magnusson, Lars
Vägen till fabrikerna. Industritraditioner och yrkeskunnande i Sverige under 1800 talet, 1983

Janson, Anders
Hundra år med svenska restaurangvagnar–deras utformning och utveckling, 1995

Jensen, Oliver
Railroads in America, 1975

Johansson, Akf
Arbetsrörelsen och Taylorismen, 1990

Julihn, Eric
Industriminnen i Mullsjö kommun, 1977

Kälvemark, Ann Sofie, red.
Utvandring. Den svenska emigrationen till Amerika i historisk perspektiv. En antologi, 1973

Kosik, Karel
Det konkretas dialektik. En studie i människans och världens problematik, 1978

Linde, Bjur
Stationshus 1855-1895. A.W. Edelsvärd som järnvägsarkitekt, 1989

Lindell, Arthur G.
School Section Sixteen, 1983

Lindsey, Almont
The Pullman Strike. Story of a unique experiment and of a great labor upheaval, 1942 (1964)

Liedman, Sven-Erik
I skuggan ov framtiden, modernitetens idéhistoria, 1998

Lindqvist, Mats
Klasskamrater, 1987

Lindälv, Elof
Klippans kulturreservat och andra byggnadsminnen i Majorna, 1977

Ljungmark, Lars
Den stora utvandringen. Svensk emigration till USA 1840-1925, 1965

Martin, A.
Railroads Triumphant. The Growth, Rejection, and Rebirth of a Vital American Force, 1992

Miller, Donald
City of the Century, 1996

Nilson, Allan T.
Mottaglighet för de nya idéerna. I Småländska Kulturbilder 1962

Nilson, Allan T.
New Sweden, Maine, förändringar och karakteristika hos svenskättlingar under jämförelse med några andra etniska grupper i Nord-Östamerika. I Unda Maris 1975

Nilson. Allan T.
Svenskt i New England, särskilt i New Britain, en kulturmötesstudie, 1988

Norborg, Lars-Arne
Svensk samhällsutveckling 1809-1979, 1980

Nordahl, Per
De sålde sina penslar, om några svenska målare som emigrerade till USA, 1987

Norman, Hans-Runblom Harald
Transatlantic Connections, 1987

North, Douglas C.
Growth and Welfare in American Past, 1996

Nothin, Erik
Vagnlära. På uppdrag af Kungl. Järnvägsstyrelsen, 1880-1920, 1990

Olson, Anita R.
The Community Created: Chicago Swedes 1880-1920, 1990

Olson, Anita R.
Swedish Chicago: The extension and Transformation of an Urban Immigrant Community, 1886-1920, 1996

Otterbjörk, Roland
Svenska förnamn. Kortfattat namnlexikon, 1964

Owen, Robert
A New View of Society and other writings, 1991, (1813-1816)

Palm, August
Ögonblicksbilder från en tripp till Amerika, 1901

Rosenau, Helen
The Ideal City, 1969

Rossberg, Ralf Roman
Geschichte der Eisenbahn, 1977

Rygert, Göran
Svenska arkitekter i USA 1846-1930, 1996

Sager, Robert
Ryfors bruk. Självbiografiska anteckningar från barn-och ungdomsåren, 1992.
Utg. Bengt Berglund och Bengt O.T. Sjögren

von Schéele Gez. K.H.
Hemlandstoner. En hälsning från moder Svea till dotterkyrkan i Amerika, 1894-95

Skarin Frykman, Birgitta
Mat och måltider. Bland arbetare och tjänstemän i Jonsered under 1900-talet, 1976

Skarin Frykman, Birgitta
Arbetarkultur–Göteborg, 1990

Statens Järnvägar 1856-1906
Teknisk Economisk Beskrivning. Red. Gustaf Welin, 1906

Swedish-American Life in Chicago
Ed. Philip J. Andersson-Dag Blanck, 1991

Thompson, E.P.
The Making of the English Working Class, 1961

Tiedemann, Christian
Minnen från Margreteholm, 1996

Waldenström, P.
Genom Norra Amerikas Förinta Stater, 1891

Warlegg-Hesse van E.
Nord-Amerika i våra dagar, 1880

Westin, Gunnar
Emigranterna och kyrkan, brev från och till svenskar i Amerika 1849-1892, 1932
Vetenskap som vardag, 1996

White, John H.
The American Railroad Passenger Car, 1978

Widmalm, Sven
Chicago steg ur askan. I Svenska Dagbladet, 1996 10 13

Wrangel, F.U.
Strövtåg i New York och annorstädes, 1907

Supplement
Emigrants From Nykyrke Parish 1850-1910

LIST OF PERSONS

Origin	Year	Name	Occupation
Björkäng	1897	Klas Adolf Knut Ljungström Returned 1912	son
Bosebygd	1852	Gustaf Johansson Lundin	farm hand
	1869	Hilda Christina Andersdotter	daughter
	1867	Johan August Andersson	laborer
	1863	Karl Victor Andersson	son
	1863	Inga Catarina Gustafsdotter	maid
	1893	Jenny Lovisa Toll	maid
Alunda	1882	Karl Gustav Lindblom	road worker
	1882	Oliva Benjaminsdotter	wife
	1882	Hugo Natanael	son
	1882	Karl Olivo	son
	1882	Lydia Maria	daughter
	1889	Anna Sofia Andersdotter (Mexico)	seamstress
Aronsdal	1892	Johan Alfrid Aronsson	farm hand
	1895	Karl Victor Aronsson (home 1899)	son
Hultet	1881	Johan Gotfrid Andersson Bolin	married man
	1886	Matilda Charlotta Andersdotter	wife
	1886	John Sigfrid	sou
	1886	Gustaf Theodor Bolin	farm hand
Cottage	1889	Anna Maria Svantesson	wife
in Hultet	1889	Oskara Josefina	daughter
	1889	Johan Edvard	son
	1889	Johan Alfrid Valdemar	son
	1889	Nils Gustaf Svante	son
	1889	Karl Oskar Hugo	son
Bredared	1861	Julia Fröding	housewife
	1867	Josefina Carlsdotter	maid
	1881	Ada Josefina Carlsdotter	maid
	1882	Axel Emil Larsson	son
	1883	Lars Albin Larsson	son
	1888	Erik Waldemar Larsson	son
Broberg	1888	Karl Johan Svansson Bro	farm hand

	1891	Hilma Maria Karlsdotter Bro	daughter
Bråred	1864	Johan Kjellander	home owner
	1864	Johanna Carlsdotter	wife
	1864	Emma Christina	daughter
	1864	Claes Alfrid	son
	1864	Anna Fredrika	daughter
Bäckebostuga	1852	Adam Larsson	man
	1852	Maria Gustavsdotter	wife
Ekeled	1886	Claes Emil Lager	smith
	1892	Emma Sofia Lager	wife
	1892	Eva Emilia	daughter
Erlandshemmet	1908	Gustav Vitalis Karlsson	son
Ersered	1881	Petronella Bergsdotter	dairy maid
	1890	Hilda Josefina Lundstedt	maid
	1891	Karl Rickard Karlsson (Returned 1897)	servant
	1893	Axel Ulrik Theodor Rofengren	servant
	1894	Josefina Andersdotter	maid
	1902	Rickard Vilhelm Boström	farm hand
	1902	Ernst Hjalmar Åkerberg	son
Flyttered	1883	Gustaf Andersson	farm hand
Granbäck	1887	Emma Christina Enochson	maid
	1886	Adina Sofia Enochson	maid
	1890	Selma Octavia Enochson	maid
	1890	Therosina Borghilda Enochson	maid
	1890	Frans Rudolf Enochson	farm hand
	1891	Frans August Nilsson	son
	1899	Teresia Borghilda (returned 1903)	maid
	1892	Karl Johan Nilsson (returned 1895)	farm hand
Berget	1852	Carl Fredrik Forsberg	laborer
Granstugan	1889	Johanna Andersdotter	household widow
Gunnarsbo	1887	Ottilia Kristina Svantesdotter	maid
	1885	Anna Maria Svantesdotter	maid
	1887	Karl Rickard Svanteson	son
	1881	Pär Otto Gustafsson	farm hand
	1902	Karl Viktor Gustafson	farm hand
Framås	1890	Karl Johan Gustaf Lindqvist	tailor

	1890	Signe D Eleonora	daughter
Gylgeryd	1869	Johan Wilhelm Andersson	farm hand
	1875	Per August Andersson	farm hand
	1881	Karl Gustaf Andersson	youth
	1890	Claes Emil Johansson	farm hand
Lilla Gålleryd	1881	Karl Gustaf J Gren	former soldier
Åsen	1881	Mathilda Carolina Jonsdotter	wife
	1881	Anna Elsibet	daughter
	1893	Johan A Karlsson Ljunqvist	former soldier
	1893	Klara Gustava Johansdotter Wahl	wife
	1893	Beda Maria	daughter
	1893	Karl Johan	son
	1893	Elin Elisabeth	daughter
	1893	Gerda Victoria	daughter
	1893	Klara Lovisa Ingeborg	daughter
Stora Gålleryd	1889	Tekla Josefina Carlsdotter	maid
Enebacken	1883	August Enström	journeyman tailor
Kullen	1890	Karl Gottfrid Andersson	farm hand
Mullsjö	1869	Maria Andersdotter	maid
	1881	August Viktor Eriksson	farm hand
	1887	Johan Oskar Svantesson	working man
	1888	August Örn	working smith
	1889	Ella Lovisa Susanna Örn	wife
	1889	Axel Georg	son
	1889	Karl Hugo	son
	1892	Johanna Kristina Lindqvist	wife
	1892	Ada Josefina (father, see Framås)	daughter
	1892	Ester Albina	daughter
	1892	Vendela Emilia Kristina	daughter
	1892	Adina Kornelia	daughter
	1892	Anny Vahlborg	daughter
	1902	Anna Lovisa Svantesdotter	daughter
	1907	Paul Sigfrid Jakobsson	son
Halvstenshult Björkelund	1869	Johannes Gustafsson	tenant farmer
	1882	David Andersson	farm hand
	1869	Claes Magnus Wilh Gustafsson	farm hand
	1869	Sven Andersson	cow house baliff
	1869	Christina Svensdotter	wife

	1869	Matilda Christina	daughter
	1869	Frans Gustaf	son
	1869	Frida Sofia	daughter
	1869	Jenny	daughter
	1869	Thekla Ottilia	daughter
	1887	Karl Gustaf Andersson	farm hand
	1887	Anna Olivia Persdotter	maid
Hofmantorp	1895	Josef Thorolf Sandén (Levinsson)	son
Höryd	1863	Axel Andersson	son
	1864	Karl Johan Zachrisson	lessee
	1902	Anna Lovisa Johansson	daughter
Lagmansered	1865	Hans Blixt	working man
	1865	Maja C Asp	wife
	1865	Johan Linus	son
	1886	Johan Gottfrid Ansersson	farm hand
Mabacken	1867	Lotta Jacobsdotter	maid
	1869	Carl Levin Brunskog	son
Maholm	1869	Frithiof Alexis Engström	tanner
	1870	Alex Engström	tanner
Olofsdal	1892	Aron Gottfrid Andersson	painter
	1892	Augusta Ros	wife
	1892	Gunnar	son
Ryds kvarn	1900	Frans Augustssou	son
	1903	Nelly Kristina Josefsson	daughter
Ryfors	1889	Ivar Viktoe Zelander	son
	1887	Per Aron Schulz	son
	1890	Karl Ulrik Forsberg	smith worker
	1890	Kristina Amalia	maid
	1886	Adolf Fredrik Eklund	smith worker
	1890	Karl Johan Örn	smith worker
	1895	Albert Emanuel Engberg	accountant
	1898	Gustaf Robert Åkerberg	son
	1893	Carl Gustaf Forsberg	smith
	1893	Stina Lovisa Persdotter	wife
	1893	Seth August	son
	1893	Hedvig Mariana	daughter
	1893	Axel Martin	son
	1893	Arvid Egidius	son
	1893	Anna Elvira	daughter
	1900	Helfrid Anna Elisabeth Södergren	daughter

	1895	Maria Kristina Jaensson Södergren	maid
	1892	Aron Augustsson (Jönsson)	farm hand
	1901	August Henrik Hurtig	son
	1901	Gertrud Sofia Södergren	daughter
	1905	Fritz Bernhard Johansson	son
	1905	Erik Olof Johansson	son
	1906	Karl Reinhold Hurtig	son
Rosenborg	1897	Anna Kristina Landgren	maid
Sjöryd	1869	Gustaf Svensson	lessee
	1869	Frans Wilhelm J Sjöberg	railroad worker
Sjövik	1892	Johan Gottfrid Skog	smith
	1892	Hedda Johansdotter	wife
	1892	Tham Gottfrid	son
Skogslund	1898	Anna Josefina Svenningsdotter	daughter
Skogshemmet	1888	Hedda Falk	widow
Spångerna	1893	Anders Johan Karlsson (returned 1895)	farm hand
Stationen	1871	Anna Kristina Johansdotter	maid
	1867	Lotta Sofia Abrahamsdotter	maid
	1892	Gustaf Ansgarius Jarl	farm hand
	1898	Signe Maria Alva Vik	daughter
Stenhult	1891	Ester Kristina Bolin	illegitimate child
Stranden	1892	Karl Albin Forsell	youth
Sörarps kvarn	1881	Johan Wilhelm Hellström	miller
	1882	Oskar Reinhold Hellström	miller
	1889	Hulda A. Hellström	maid
	1888	Anna Emilia Hellström	maid
	1888	Gustaf Fingal Hellström	son
	1891	August Fritiof Hellström	youth
	1900	David Alfrid Hellström	son
	1903	Helena Maria Hellström	daughter
	1903	Anders Filip Hellström	son
	1906	Karl Alfred Hellström (returned 1906)	miller
Sörarp	1889	Karl Robert Severin	youth
	1889	Gustaf Wilhelm Severin	youth
	1899	Johannes Gustafsson Severin	tailor
	1899	Johanna Elisabeth Schulz	wife
	1898	Knut Filemon	son
	1899	Emma Sofia	daughter

	1899	Jacob Vilgot	son
	1901	Karl Axel Hurtig	son
	1902	Karl Fritiof Josefsson	smith worker
Soldattorp	1887	Karl Alfrid Ragnar	farm hand
Blankebacka	1890	Lisen Mathilda Carlsson	maid
	1895	Hilma Vilhelmina Karlsdotter	daughter
	1910	Isak Natanael Lilja	son
Utterhaga	1900	Karl Axel Gottfrid Johansson	shoemaker
	1906	Johan Arvid Utterberg	son
Wasen	1901	Kasper Emanuel Gustafsson	son

Total emigrants 1850-1910–200 persons.

This list was compiled by Bengt Berglund, Göteborg, 11/10/1975

Index

----, Ada Josefina 117 Adina Kornelia 117 Anna Elvira 118 Anny Vahlborg 117 Arvid 12 Arvid Egidius 118 August 11 40 Aunt Fiffi 48 Axel Martin 118 Beda Maria 117 Clara 40 Dahl 40 Elin Elisabeth 117 Emma Sofia 119 Ester Albina 117 Filip 11 Fina 40 Frans Gustaf 118 Fredrik 40 Frida Sofia 118 Gerda Victoria 117 Gunnar 118 Hedvig Mariana 118 Helena 11-12 Hulda 11 Ida 11 Jacob Vilgot 120 Jenny 118 Johan 118 John 40 Karl 11 Karl Johan 117 Klara Lovisa Ingeborg 117 Knut Filemon 119 Lamberg 40 Matilda Christina 118 Mia 11 Modig 11 Otto 40 Robert 11 40 Seth August 118 Severin 13 Tham Gottfrid 119 Thekla Ottilia 118 Vendela Emilia Kristina 117
ABRAHAMSDOTTER, Lotta Sofia 119
ACLAND, Henry 2
ACTION, Ed 81
ADAMS, R H 82
ADERBERG, Ruben 30
ADLER, Dankmar 91
ADOLF, Gustav 46
ÅGREN, 29 Kurt Robert 26 Lars 46
AHLBERG, 29-30 August 26 Magnus 26
AHNLUND, Mats 71 75 102
AHNQUIST, G 32
ÅKERBERG, 26 40-41 103 (Ernest) 4 9 Albert 93 98 Arnold 93 98 Cark Johan 13 Carl 21 Emma 21 Emma Sofia 13 Ernest 12 92-93 98-99 Ernest Hjalmar 13 Ernst 4-5 9-10 13 18 21-22 24 45 49 51 92 Ernst Hjalmar 10 42 116 Gustaf Robert 42 118 Helena 13 Helene 92-93 Ida 10 12 John 10 12-13 Kenneth 93 98 Margaret (Peggy) 93 Mia 49 Tage 4 9 13 21-22 46 54 98 907
ÅKERBERGS, 31 39 43
ALFRID, Claes 116
ALLÉN, Sture 28
ALM, G T 25
ALTGELD, John P 77
AMALIA, Kristina 118
AMBJÖRNSSON, Ronny 29
ANDERSDOTTER, Anna Sofia 115 Hilda Christina 115 Johanna 116 Josefina 116 Maria 117 Matilda Charlotta 115
ANDERSON, Anton B 75 Felix 80 Fredrik Walter 30 Henoch 75 John E 31 Matilda 26 Philip J 1
ANDERSSON, A G 43 Albin 7 Aron Gottfrid 118 August 75 Axel 41 118 Britta Maria 13 David 117 Family 18 Gustaf 116 Johan 13 Johan August 115 Johan Gottfrid 41 118 Johan Wilhelm 117 Karl Gottfrid 117 Karl Gustaf 117-118 Karl Victor 115 Lindoff 59 Matilda 7 Otto 47 Per August 117 Sven 41
ANDREASSON, Johannes 15 Severina 15
ARMOUR, Philip Danforth 70 Phillip 91
ARONSSON, Johan Alfred 42 Johan Alfrid 115 Karl Victor 42 115
ARVASTSON, Gösta 33 907
ASP, Maja C 118
ASTON, B 82
ATTERBURY, G 2
AUGUST, Peter 26
AUGUSTSSON, Frans 42 45 118
AUGUSTSSON (JÖNSSON), Aron 119
AURELIUS, Harry 81 Henry 76 Mrs James 30
AUSTIN, Alice Constance 55
AXELL, Åke 41-43
BALDWIN, M 87
BALL, Harry 81 Horace 81
BALSTER, Wm 82
BARNET, Henrietta 2
BARRET, Nathan F 2 71
BARTON, H Arnold 68
BECKMAN, Mary 30
BEHRENDS, George 86
BEIJBOM, Ulf 1-2 30 907
BEMAN, S Spencer 71 Solon 34 Solon Spencer 2 56 60-61
BENANDER, 29 A M 92 Carl Albin 26 Hulda 92
BENGTSSON, Maria Carolina 25
BENJAMINSDOTTER, Oliva 115
BENSON, Family 93
BENSONS, 31
BERG, Erick 31
BERGER, J V 29
BERGGREN, 29 Hans Petter 26
BERGLUND, B 52 Bengt 40-41 120 907
BERGSDOTTER, Petronella 116
BERGSTRÖM, Josef 9
BERGSTRÖMS, 31
BILSTRAND, Gillie 76
BJUR, Gunilla Linde 60 907 Linde 63

BLACKETT, Christopher 86
BLANCHE, August 67
BLANCK, Dag 1 33
BLIXT, Hans 118
BLOMBERG, Charles 32
BLOOM, A Gustaf 65 74 Gustaf 25
BLOOMQUIST, E C 24
BOLIN, Ester Kristina 42 119 Gustaf Theodor 41 115 Johan Gotfrid Andersson 115
BOLM, 26
BONNIER, Albert 85
BORÉN, Sten Otto 26
BORGHILDA, Teresia 116
BÖRJESSON, Erik 59
BORK, Oscar 31
BOSTROM, Rickard Vilhelm 116
BOURDIEU, Pierre 91
BOWEN, James H 2 85
BOYD, Frank L 79
BRANDT, August 8 Charlie 76
BRISSMAN, Gustaf Albert 44
BRO, Augusta 44 Axel Einar 43 Beda Linnea 43 Carl Johan 43 Ellen Kristina 43 Ernst Vilger 43 Hilma Maria 43-44 Hilma Maria Karlsdotter 116 Inga Maria 43 Karl Johan Svansson 115
BRODIN, G 32
BROLING, Anders Johan 26
BROOKS, James 86
BROS, Carl 41
BRUNNER, Vera 39
BRUNNSTRÖM, Anhlund 6 Lasse 71 75 102 907
BRUNSKOG, Carl Levin 43 118
BRYLLA, Eva 29
BUDER, S 55
BURNHAM, 70 Daniel 71 Daniel H 91
BUTCHER, Ed 82
CAMPELL, Henry 86
CARLING, Henrik 1
CARLQUIST, Axel 87
CARLSDOTTER, Johanna 116 Josefina 115 117 Tekla Josefina
CARLSON, Albert E 30 Axel F N 31 Carl A 75 E O 30 Herbert (the Wall) 76 Linus 31 Ludvig 31 Nils G 30 Oscar 31 Oscar L 30 R 13
CARLSONS, 31
CARLSSON, Lisen Mathilda 120 Ture 9 Uno 40
CARNEGIE, 59 Andrew 72 David Jr 58 David Jr 2
CHRISTINA, Emma 116
CLEVELAND, President Grover 77 78
COLEMAN, McAlister 77
COOKE, Tom 81
CORNELL, Elias 71
CRAWFORD, Joan 80

CRONON, William 70
CROWTHER, H 82
CUMMINGS, Wm 82
D'ERAMO, Marco 91-92
DAHLBACKA, Ingvar 102-103
DAHLBERG, Erik 46 Mrs Gothard 30
DAHLGREN, F A 67
DAHLIN, Oscar 76 81
DARLEY, Gillian 2 55-56
DEBS, Eugene V 77-79 83
DEGEER, Eric 45
DICKSON, Walter 65-66
DISRAELI, 56
DIXON, E H 82
DOMEY, Bernhard 31
DOTY, Mrs Duane 88-89
DRIPPS, Isaac 86
EDELSVÄRD, A W 58 60 64 89
EDSTRÖM, Sigfrid 86
EDVARD, Johan 115
EISENHART, Woodrow W 4 9
EISERMAN, 40 P V 44
EK, Sven B 5
EKEBERG, G A 30
EKFELDT, Axel 7
EKLUND, Adolf Fredrik 118
ELEONORA, Signe D 117
ELFMAN, Mrs 40
ELSIBET, Anna 117
EMILIA, Eva 116
ENGBERG, 40 Albert Emanuel 118
ENGER, H 32
ENGERTH, Wilhelm 87
ENGSTRÖM, Alex 118 Alexander 41 43 Frank 26 Frithiof Alexis 118 Fritiof 43
ENOCHSON, Emma Christina 116 Frans Rudolf 116 Selma Octavia 116 Therosina Borghilda 116
ENSTRÖM, 43 August 117
ERGO, Helen 65 74
ERICKSON, A G 40 Abel A E 30 Frank T L 30 Hjalmar 76 N G 30
ERICSON, Christian 70 Nils 90 101
ERICSSON, John 86
ERIKSON, Bolla 104 Carl Oscar 31
ERIKSSON, 48 August Viktor 117
ERIXON, Sigurd 5
ESSEN, Fried (Krupp) 87
FALK, Hedda 119
FIELD, Benjamin 85 Benjamin C 2 Marshall 70
FISCHERSTRÖM, W 3
FISHLOW, Albert 101
FLINN, J P 82
FLYGELHOLM, Augusta Mathilda 44

FOCK, Ida 39
FOGEL, Robert 101
FORD, Henry 33 92 Henry J 77
FORSBERG, Carl Fredrik 41-42 116 Carl Gustaf 118 Carl Ulrik 44 G 30 Karl Gustaf 44 Karl Ulrik 118
FORSELL, Karl Albin 42 119
FRANZÉN, Luther 47
FREDRIKA, Anna 116
FRIDELL, 29 Johan Larsson 26 John 75
FRÖDING, Julia 42 115
FRÖJD, Richard 8
FRÖJERED, 48
FROMÉN, E T 24
FRYKMAN, Birgitta Skarin 59
FURULAND, Lars 67
GARDELL, Axel 8 Per 8
GELKNER, Stefan 907
GEORG, Axel 117
GERMUNDSON, Johannes 26
GIBSON, William 58 William G 2nd 59 William G 3rd 59
GJELLSTEDT, 30
GORDON, Scorer C 82
GOVIER, B 82
GRANT, Thomas 57 60
GREN, Karl Gustaf 117
GROVER, Oliver Denton 61
GULLANDER, Johan 44
GULLBERG, Gustaf 68 70
GUSTAF, Johan Anton 26
GUSTAFSDOTTER, Inga Catarina 115
GUSTAFSON, Adrian 31 Carl 31 Eric B 30 Karl Viktor 116
GUSTAFSSON, Claes Magnus Wilh 117 Johannes 117 Kasper Emanuel 120 Par Otto 116
GUSTAVSDOTTER, Maria 116
GUSTAVSSON, Arvid 8
GYLLING, Arvid 92
HAAG, J 87
HAARDY, Augsburg 87
HABERLEIN, 87
HAGMAN, S J 76
HAKANSON, Alfred 25
HAMMAR, Hugo 86
HAMMARSKIÖLD, Hans 63
HAMMOND, George H 91
HANSDOTTER, Britta Maria 13 Helena 14
HARD, 29 Alma Christina 26 Augusta Margareta 26 Bertha Matilda 26 Carl Gustaf Adolf 26 Charlotta 26 Elizabeth 26 Emma Louisa 26 Gustaf Magnus 26 Helena Maria 26 Ida Victoria 26 Matilda 26
HARDING, Warren G 93
HASSELBERG, 70

HASWELL, John 86
HATCH, Clarence 81
HAYDEN, Dolores 2 55
HEDBERG, Alexander Stefanus 14 Anna 14 Arthur 17 Frans 67 Johannes 14 Maria 14 Maria Christina 26 Sigurd 17
HEDIN, Gustaf F 75
HELGE, Ernst 31 Jan 33 Janice 29 36 905
HELLBERG, 70
HELLSTRÖM, 29 40 Anders Filip 42 119 Anna Emilia 42 119 August Fritiof 42 119 Carl 92 David 94 David Alfrid 42 119 Edward 94 Filip 12 Fritiof 12 26 94 G Fingal 39 40 Gustaf Fingal 26 41 119 Gustav 48 Helena 13 21 Helena Maria 42 119 Helene 92 94 Hulda 92 Hulda A 42 119 Johan Wilhelm 41 45 119 John 94 Karl Afred 119 Karl Alfred 12 94 Karl Edvard 41 Nils 41 Oscar 94 Oskar Reinhold 41 119 Phillip 94 Pontus 5 48 94 Reinhold 93
HELLSTRÖMS, 31 39 43
HELMHOLZ, 87
HENRICSON, Ingvar 86
HENRY, James 77
HILDEBRAND, Mrs 30
HILLSTRÖM, Armour 49 51 Clara 49 D Armour 94 David 22 49 51 94 David A 40 Edward 22 51 Family 18 Filip 22 Fingal 22 51 93-94 Fritiof 10-11 22 24 51 Johan 12 22 51 Mike 22 O R 30 Phillip 51 Pontus 22 Reinhold 12 22 51
HODELL, Frans 67
HOLABIRD, William 92
HOLES, James 2
HOLM, 40 Levin 48
HOLMBERG, Åke 90 101
HOLMS, Levin 49
HORYD, Hedda Zackrisson 42
HUGHES, Rev T 82
HUGO, Karl 117 Karl Oskar 115
HULT, Jan 907
HULTGREN, J E 66
HURTIG, 12 40-41 August 10 22 40 August Henrik 42 45 119 Emma Sofia 13 Family 18 Johan August 45 Karl 10 22 43 Karl Axel 42 120 Karl Reinhold 42 45 119 Reinhold 93 Robert 48-49
HURTIGS, 39 43
JACOBSDOTTER, Lotta 118
JACOBSON, W F 24
JAKOBSSON, Paul Sigfrid 117
JANSDOTTER, Anna Sofia 44
JANSON, Karl 18
JANSSON, Karl 11
JARL, Gustaf Ansgarius 119
JARLERT, Anders 102
JENNY, William Le Baron 91

JENSEN, Oliver 96
JOHANNESSON, Anders Samuel 15 Anna 16-17 Carl Herman 16 Carl Otto 15-16 Fasta 17 Frida 4 Gustaf 16-17 Johan Algot 15 Nils Gustaf 4 15
JÖHANSDOTTER, Anna Kristina 119 Anna Stina 45 Eva 43 Hedda 119 Lisa 45
JOHANSSON, Anna Josefina Hedberg 13 Anna Lovisa 118 Börje 907 Carl Herman 13-14 Claes Emil 117 Erik Olof 119 Fritz Bernhard 119 Gustaf 14 Gustaf Adolph 13 Ingrid (Faster Ida) 14 Jonas Petter 24 Karl Axel Gottfrid 42 120
JOHNSON, Albin 31 Anna 17 Anna Hedberg 34 Anna W 24 Axel Fridolf 25 Carl 31 Charlotta 25 Emma Augusta Charlotta 25 Florence Victoria 25 Gust J 14 62 Gustaf J 4 Henry 25 Hjalmar 14 Hulda Theresia 25 Johan D 31 Lillian 17 Pehr August 25 R E 35 Raymond 14 Raymond E 4 13 15-19 24 62-63 80 103 905 907 Verner 31 Victor Rudolf 25 Warren 17 105
JOHNSONS, 31
JOHNSTON, W A 102
JONASSON, Pastor 24
JONSDOTTER, Mathilda Carolina 117 Severina 14-16
JONSON, Charles August 75
JONSSON, 40 (Jöss Anna) 47 August 45 Karl (Jösskarl) (Jösse) 47
JORGENSEN, Karl 1
JOSEFINA, Oskara 115
JOSEFSSON, Karl Fritiof 120 Nelly 42 Nelly Kristina 118
JUHLIN, Eric 46
KÄNSTRÖM, 29 Anna Katarina 26 Paulus 26
KARLSDOTTER, Hilma Maria 42 Hilma Vilhelmina 120
KARLSON, E 25 74
KARLSSON, Anders Johan 43 119 E 65 Gustav Vitalis 116 Karl Rickard 116 Kurt 93 Martin 8 Oscar 8 104
KEILLER, Alexander 58
KEMAN, Oscar 58
KINDLUND, Per 40
KJELLANDER, Carl 36 Johan 41 116
KONRAD OF GRANBACK, 49
KRAUSS, 87
KREUGER, 70
KRUPP, 92
KULLANDER, B 3
KUNST, George 81
KUYLENSTIERNA, Capt 10
LAGER, Claes 43 Claes Emil 116 Emma Sofia 116
LAGERHOLM, 28 Ivar 26
LANDERHOLM, Edvard 42 44

LANDGREN, Anna Kristina 119
LANE, Kerstin 102
LARSON, Charles A 30 Elmer Th 30 Fanny Mia Elisabeth 25 Gerda 25 Harold C L 30 Hilma Sofia 25 Lars Peter 25
LARSSON, Adam 41-42 116 Axel Emil 115 Bud 9 Carl 70 Erik Waldemar 115 Lars Albin 115 Nels O 40
LEMAN, 26 28
LENANDER, 29 Gustaf Julius Artur 26
LETOUX, J P R 39
LEVER, William H 2
LEVIN, Carl 41
LILJA, Isak Natanael 120
LILJEFORS, 70
LILLIEHÖÖK, H 87
LINCOLN, President 92
LIND, Arvid 47 Signe 47
LINDÄLV, Elov 60
LINDBLAD, H G 30 Hans 86
LINDBLOM, Karl Gustav 115
LINDELL, 29 Anton W 31 Karl Johan 26
LINDGREN, Carl A 30
LINDH, Erik 8
LINDQUIST, 74 Mr 30
LINDQVIST, Johanna Kristina 117 Karl Johan Gustaf 116
LINDSEY, Almont 56 77
LINDSKOG, Axel 76
LINN, Björn 907
LINTLEMAN, Joy K 68
LJUNGBLAD, Ida 93
LJUNGMARK, Lars 30 907
LJUNGQVIST, 48
LJUNGSTRÖM, Clas Johan 42 Klas Adolf Knut 42 115
LJUNQVIST, Johan A Karlsson 117
LOCKWOOD, 56
LÖFGREN, John G 30
LÖNNQUIST, Sigrid Christina 26
LÖÖF, Lars Olof 907
LORENT, A R 58
LOWE, J B 2
LUND, Arvid 76 David A 30
LUNDAHL, Charles 76
LUNDBERG, 65 74 Benjamin 30 Jennie 30
LUNDELL, Carl A 26
LUNDGREN, Carl Otto 9
LUNDIN, Gustaf Johansson 41 115 John 32
LUNDKVIST, Artur 103
LUNDSTEDT, Hilda Josefina 116
LYCKBERG, P J D 24
MALAK, Paula 33

MALMSTEN, Erik 907
MALMSTRÖM, 65 74
MANN, W D 85-86
MARIA, Lydia 115
MARTIN, Albro 101
MAWSON, 56
MCQUEEN, George 81
MCWATT, Arthur C 79
MEAKINS, B 2
MELLIN, K J 87
MESTERSTON, Ingrid 59
MILLER, Donald L 70-71 907
MOLIN, 29 Gustaf Adolf 26
MOLTKE-HUITFELDT, Marie 39
MORÉN, 29 Anders Gabriel Kristofferson 26
MÖRNER, Berndt Diedric 46
MUREEN, Axel 24
MYRÉN, Nils Nilsson 26
NAGELMACKERS, Georges 85
NATANAEL, Hugo 115
NELSON, Ingrid Carolina 14
NEVIN, Allan 77
NILSON, Allan T 120 905 Björn 907 Brita 907 Erik 907 Henrik 907 Tove 907
NILSSON, Frans August 116 Karl Johan 116 Werner 47
NORBORG, Lars-Arne 90
NORDAHL, Per 67
NORDELL, Carl 32
NORDIN, Sven 76
NORDLUND, Henry 9
NORDLUNDS, 31
NORDQVIST, David E 9
NORDSTRAND, Eric 9
NORDSTRANDS, 31
NORDSTRÖM, 70
NORLIN, Harry 9
NORLING, Family 18
NORLINS, 31
NORRMAN, A J 32 Karin 28 Sven 28
NORRSTRÖM, 29
NORSTRÖM, Carl Peter Hugo 26
NORTH, Douglas C 90 101
NOTHIN, G 3
NYLANDER, Florence 30
NYMAN, 29 Gustaf Harry 26
NYSTRÖM, 70 Grete 8
ÖHMAN, Helena Elizabeth 24
OKERBERG, Joshua 99 Paul 93 99
OLIVO, Karl 115
OLMSTED, Frederick Law 102 Fredrik Law 71 John Charles 102
OLNEY, Richard 77-78

OLSON, Anita R 1-2 68 102 Anita Ruth 5 Carl Emil 31 Harriet 30 Ivar Carl 30 John 59 K August 8 O 25 Tage 31
OLSSON, Karl A 29
OMAN, John 24
ORN, August 117 Ella Lovisa Susanna 117 Karl Johan 118
ORNE, Albert 81
OSBECK, Anna Greta 44
OTTERBJÖRK, Roland 28
OWEN, Robert 2
PALM, August 1 67
PAULSEN, Julius R 30
PEARSON, 65 74 Ludvig 31
PEARSONS, 31
PERSDOTTER, Anna Olivia 118 Stina Lovisa 44 118
PERSON, Anders Vilhelm 26 Gustaf 75
PERSSON, Folke F 9 Gunnar 76 Lennart K 907
PETERSON, Amanda Laurentia 25 Andrew 25 Anna 76 Arvid Pontus 25 B 76 Ebba Christina 25 Erik Mattias 25 Gottfried Ferdinand 30 Johan Henning 25 Maria Carolina 25 Swan 32
PETTERSSON, Ivar 47 Sven 43
PHILPOTT, F 82 J 82
PIHL, Eric 9 Hanna 9
PULLMAN, 59-60 (Lolita) 94 Florence 71 G M 3 33 70 72 78 86 94-95 907 909-910 George 9 56 71 George M 2 34 77 92 George Mortimer 2 7 20 55 57-58 79 85 101 Harriet 71
RÄF, Emil 40
RAGNAR, Gustaf 44 Karl Alfred 41 44 Karl Alfrid 120
RANDOLPH, Philip 79-80
RAPP, 29 Anders Gustaf 26 Carl J 26
REHNBERG, Bertil 907
REPS, John W 102
RICHARDSON, 87 Henry Hobson 92
RIGGENBACH, Nikolaus 87
RINGMAN, 40
ROBERTS, Henry 2
ROFENGREN, Axel Ulrik Theodor 116
ROMAN, R R 96
ROOSEVELT, Franklin D 80
ROOT, John W 91 John Wellborn 71
ROS, Agusta 118
ROSENAU, Helen 2 55-56
ROSENIUS, 30
RÖSSEL, 78
ROWNTREE, Joseph 2
RUNBLOM, Harald 68
SAGER, Countess Marie 49 Edvard 39 41 46 49 G M 41 John Henry 46 49 Leo 39 44 51 Lt 40

SAGER (cont.)
    Maria Moltke 40 Marie 39 Mrs 40 Robert 39 41
    52 Vera 39 51
SAGERS, 43
SAHLBERG, Ernst 8
SALBORN, Marianne 8
SALT, Sir Titus 56-57 92
SAMUELSSON, August 40
SANDBURG, Carl 103
SANDÉN, Josef Thorulf (Tore) 42 Thorulf 43
SANDÉN (LEVINSSON), Josef Thorolf 118
SANDSTEDT, Mia 12
SANDSTRÖM, 29 Carl A 25 Carl August 26
    Samuelsson Frans Alfred 26 Sven Erland 26
SCHIVELBUSCH, Wolfgang 94
SCHÖNING, Ivar 31
SCHULTZ, Anna Greta 44 Gustaf 42 Jacob 44
    Johanna Elisabeth 44 Per Anders 41 Peter 40
SCHULZ, Johanna Elisabeth 119 Per Aron 43 118
SCOWCROFT, W 82
SEAGREN, Oscar 65 74
SEARS, Richard Warren 70
SELANDER, Doris 49 Hans Peter 30
SELIN, Frida 4 17
SELLDÉN, 29 Peter Johan Johanson 26
SEQUIN, Mare 86
SETTERDAHL, Lennart 25 32
SEVERIN, 40 Gustaf 40 Gustaf Wilhelm 42 119 Johannes Gustafsson 44 119 Karl Robert 42 44 119 Wilhelm Gustaf 44
SIEMENS, Werner 87
SIGFRID, John 115
SINATRA, Frank 80
SJÖBERG, Frans Wilhelm J 41 119 Helene 94
SJÖBLOM, Ada 26 Beda 26
SJÖGÅRD, Goran 94
SJÖGREN, Bengt O T 907
SJÖHOLM, Arvid 31
SKOG, Johan Gottfrid 119
SMALE, V J 82
SMOCK, Garrard Jr 80 Virgil 80
SÖDERGREN, 28 Anna Christina 25 Family 18
    Gerda Sofia 45 Gertrud Sofia 42 119 Helfrid
    Anna Elisabeth 42 118 Helfrida 45 Helfrida Anna
    Elisabeth 44 Hugo Evald 25 Johan Alfred Waldemar 25 Karl Oscar 44 Maria Kristina Jaensson
    119 Nanna Emilia 25 Oscar Gustaf Herbert 25
    Otto Waldemar 25 Wilhelm Otto 25
SÖDERMAN, Elisabeth 93
SPADE, Bengt 46 53-54
SPÅNG, Bror 48
SPÅNGS, 39
SPRANGERNA, Edvard Of 47

STARK, G K 24 30
STEN, (Army Name) 8 J Henrik 8 Victor Emil 8
STEPHENSON, George 86
STEVENS, John 86
STIRLING, Patrick 87
STONE, J Henrik 8 James E 8 Victor Emil 8
STORCKENFELDT, E 87
STORM, Margit Kjellander 36
STRAND, 29 Johan Magnus 26
STRÅNG, Johanna 44
STRÖM, Carl 9
STRÖMS, 31
STROUDLEY, William 87
SULLIVAN, Louis 71 91
SUNDBÅRG, Gustaf 45
SUNDBERG, Thore 76
SUNDELL, Carl 9 Gustav 9 Lilly 9 Oscar 9 Oskar 9
SUNDELLS, 31
SUNDSTRÖM, Manfred 31
SVANTE, Nils Gustaf 115
SVANTESDOTTER, Anna Lovisa 117 Anna Maria
    116 Ottilia Kristina 116
SVANTESON, Karl Rickard 116
SVANTESSON, Anna Maria 115 Johan Oskar 117
SVENNINGSDOTTER, Anna Josefina 119 Anna
    Josefine 42
SVENSDOTTER, Christina 117 Johanna 44
SVENSSON, Gustaf 41 119 Sigfrid 5
SWANSON, Carl 31 H 76 M 31 Olle 31
SWANTON, Johan 26
SWENSÉN, 29 Carl 26
SWENSON, Emil 31
TAFT, Judge 1
TEDÉN, 29 Carl Johan 26
TENGWALD, Pastor 24 V J 30
THARP, Horace 25
THOMPSON, Anna 76 August Gideon 30 Racine 76
    82
THURESON, K 25 K T 65 T K 74
TIDERMAN, 40
TIMGREN, 26
TOLIN, Carl A 31
TOLL, Family 42 Jenny Lovisa 42 115
TOPELIUS, Zackarias 67
TOPSÖE, V G S 85
TÖRNQUIST, Harry 76 Iwan 75
TÖRNQVIST, Konrad 59
TRUMAN, Harry 80
TRUMBULL, Lyman 77
TUNGREN, 29
TURNER, 87 M Jr 82
UPJOHN, Richard 56
UTTERBERG, J A 43 Johan Arvid 42 120

VALDEMAR, Johan Alfrid 115
VAN DEUTEKOM, A 82
VIBERG, Ernest 76
VIK, Signe Maria Alva 119
VON HESSE-WARTEGG, E 1
VON KOCH, G H 1
VON WALDEGG, Heusiger 87
WAHL, Klara Gustava Johansdotter 117
WAHLIN, Staffan 28
WALDENSTRÖM, P 19
WALSCHAERT, E 87
WARD, Aaron Montgomery 70
WARREN, Earl 80
WEBERG, A 76
WELIN, Gustav 87
WENNERBERG, Gunnar (Choir) 67
WENSTROM, Claus W 75
WESTIN, Gunnar 29
WESTINGHOUSE, George 87
WHITE, Horace 77 John H 97
WIDMALM, Sven 70
WIK-THORSELL, Anna-Lena 29
WILD, F 82
WINSTRÖM, Bertil G 9
WOLFF, Jim 76
WRANGEL, F U 1
WRIGHT, Frank Lloyd 71 91
YERKES, Charles Tyson 70
YOUNG, George 80
ZACHAROFF, Gunnar 59
ZACHRISSON, Karl Johan 118
ZARA, Guiseppe 87
ZELANDER, 40 Augusta Mathilda 44 Ivar Victor 42 44 Ivar Viktoe 118 Ivar Viktor 43 Johan Victor 44
ZETTERSTRAND, E A 30 Pastor 24 29 Rev 27 Ulrika Eleonora 24
ZORN, 70